Piano

Play it again

PIANO

BOOK 3

Melanie Spanswick

ED 14017

www.schott-music.com

Mainz • London • Madrid • Berlin • New York • Paris • Prague • Tokyo • Toronto

MUSICAL TERMS

Note values are given in the order American-British on their first mention within each section, then American terms alone thereafter.

whole note (semibreve)
half note (minim)
quarter note (crotchet)
eighth note (quaver)
sixteenth note (semiquaver)
thirty-second note (demisemiquaver)
sixty-fourth note (hemidemisemiquaver)

See also the table in Book 1, page 113

Other terms follow British usage, for example:
bar (Br) = measure (Am)
whole tone (Br) = whole step (Am)
semitone (Br) = half step (Am)
stave (Br) = staff (Am)

ED 14017
British Library Cataloguing-in-Publication Data.
A catalogue record for this book is available from the British Library
ISMN 979-0-2201-3810-2
ISBN 978-1-84761-495-7

Cover design by Gary Baker
Book design by Chloë Alexander Design
Photos by Matthew Ward
Back cover photo by Fabrice Rizzato
Printed in Germany S&Co.9440

Contents

From the author

Play it again: Piano is a progressive piano course consisting of graded piano pieces intended for anyone who has played the piano before and wishes to rediscover this fulfilling pastime. It is also a useful course for students of any age wishing to progress from an elementary to advanced level, whilst discovering a wealth of repertoire which is prefaced with helpful technical and musical suggestions.

Book 1 starts almost at the beginning, with a look at the musical basics, musicianship and a step-by-step guide on how to learn each piece effectively, and *Book 2* builds on this foundation taking students up to advanced level. *Book 3* continues the journey from Grade 8 up to Associate Diploma level. You could go straight to *Book 3* if you feel confident enough and you are already an experienced pianist, but I would always recommend first reviewing the fundamentals of music and piano technique in *Book 1 and 2*.

Each book contains carefully selected pieces which gradually increase in difficulty and cover a wide variety of styles and musical periods. By the end of the third book, you should be able to tackle advanced pieces comparable to the Associate Diploma standard of the leading British exam boards.

For this third book I have selected 11 piano works which I hope you will find both interesting and rewarding to play. The book is divided into two sections: Post Grade 8 Diploma and Associate Diploma level (which are approximately equivalent to the diplomas of the Associated Board of the Royal Schools of Music (ABRSM), Trinity College London and the London College of Music):

Post Grade 8 Diploma
Grade 8 level – Post Grade 8 Diploma
Associate Diploma
Post Grade 8 Diploma – Associate Diploma

In this volume we move from Grade 8 (the highest grade of amateur piano exams) on to diploma level music, which is considered similar to a standard of playing approaching a professional level. A selection of pieces to include some on the examination syllabuses has been chosen, and will hopefully inspire those considering undertaking these exams.

I have included photographs, diagrams and many musical examples to illustrate key aspects of piano technique such as hand flexibility, the Bridge position and finger strength, as well as advice on the most effective approaches to practicing. I will show you how to break pieces down in order to help tackle their technical and musical challenges. Once you have completed all three books of *Play it again: Piano* you will be able to select, analyse, practice and perform pieces with confidence and enjoy making real progress in your practice sessions.

You can also find a selection of teaching videos on YouTube available at www.youtube.com/user/SchottM.

Melanie Spanswick MMus (RCM), GRSM (Hons), DipRCM, ARCM

www.melaniespanswick.com

How to use *Play it again: Piano*

The first part of this book covers many aspects of piano technique and will serve as a resource to which you can refer when working through the rest of the book. Read these sections thoroughly: flexibility and relaxed movement at the piano are crucial for enjoyable playing. The practice tips and advice will make your time at the keyboard more effective and rewarding; keep these in mind when working through the repertoire.

MUSICAL REMINDERS

The *Practice Reminder* section at the end of this book focuses on extra beneficial material for warming-up pre-practice. It may be helpful to review this information before you dive in to work on the pieces; I recommend revisiting the warm-up exercises at the start of each practice session.

A NOTE ON REPERTOIRE

Both units in *Play it again: Piano* – Book 3 (Post Grade 8 Diploma and Associate Diploma) feature a selection of beneficial piano works; six in the Post Grade 8 Diploma unit and five in the Associate Diploma unit. Each section contains a technical study and a variety of Classical repertoire drawn from a wide range of styles to help further your technical and musical progress.

Every piece offers a different focus in terms of technique and musicianship, and is preceded by useful information including preparation tips, practice techniques, tailor-made exercises and ideas for your interpretation.

Piano technique

Posture, hand positions, flexibility and alignment

The first two volumes of this piano course place much emphasis on physical flexibility and relaxed movement at the keyboard during practice and performance. Book 3 *will continue in the same vein, with plenty of tips and exercises to encourage good posture, hand positions, and easy movement free from tension, whilst developing finger strength and fostering ideal tonal production.*

At this point it would be prudent to visit (or revisit) the technique sections at the beginning of Book 1 and 2, as they contain useful exercises and important information on keeping wrists and arms relaxed, as well as ideas to implement finger strength. There are also seven tips in Book 1 and 2 for scales, arpeggios and sight-reading practice, instigating good habits to help develop these necessary skills.

Technique becomes increasingly crucial as playing gradually improves, and more complex piano music, particularly advanced repertoire, such as that found in this book, is tackled. At this point in Book 3, we will continue to build on the technical exercises in Book 1 and 2, and examine various ways of keeping flexible at the same time as consciously developing the bridge, or hand/knuckle, position, whilst strengthening the fingers, particularly the fourth and fifth. It can be beneficial to work at these aspects separately, at the start of a practice session, mindful of observing hands, fingers and general posture during practice.

I have discussed wrist flexibility at length in the previous volumes, and hopefully you will now be implementing this important technique. Hand and arm alignment is vital, that is, the wrist and arm must not be too high or low when playing the piano (see Book 1 page 6). However, in order to hone real relaxation and flexibility, it is sometimes necessary to exaggerate movements to successfully assimilate the 'feeling' of looseness; this is especially true for those returning to playing the instrument, where tension and tautness throughout the upper body often cause issues.

Tip

In order to develop a secure piano technique, we must master the concept of tension and release; tension is required to sound notes, but as soon as they have been played, the release of the muscles involved ensures comfort and flexibility in between notes, and provides the necessary relaxed physical stance to continue playing note patterns with ease.

HAND FLEXIBILITY

Hands can easily become locked and tense, rendering playing an uncomfortable, tight experience. Wrists and arms should ideally feel soft, light and loose as we play, whilst the fingers and knuckles remain firm. But hands also need to be relaxed too, in order to open and 'reach' larger intervals with ease, such as chords and octaves. The aim should be to balance the hand so that it's possible to use the fourth and fifth finger as easily and comfortably as the thumb and second finger.

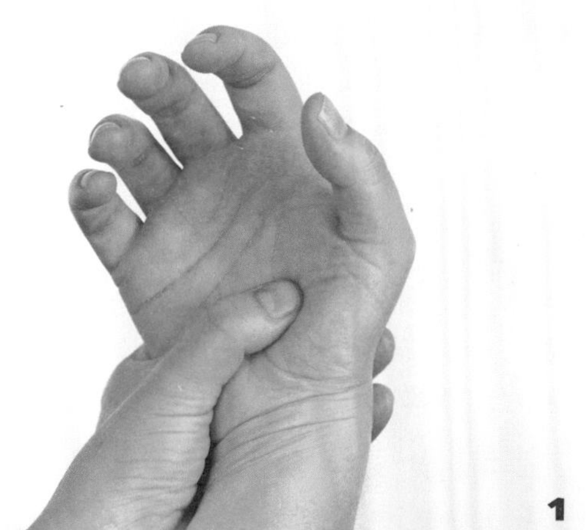

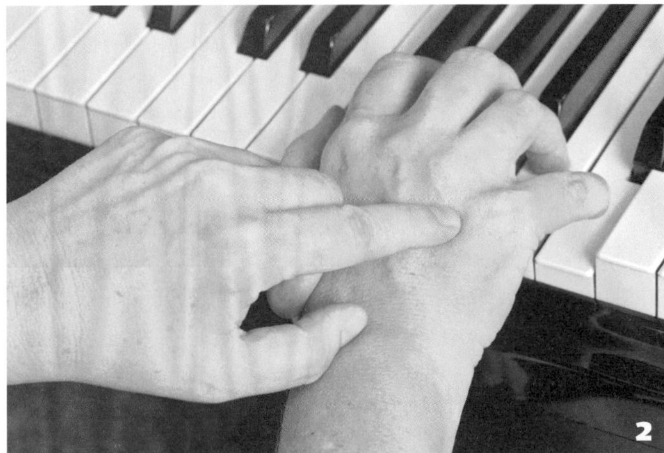

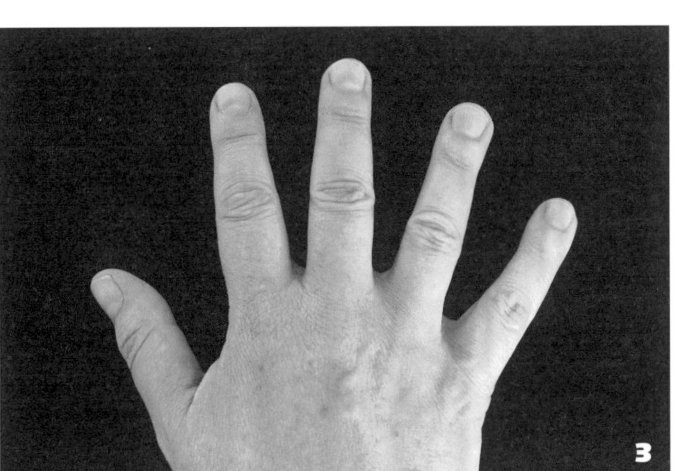

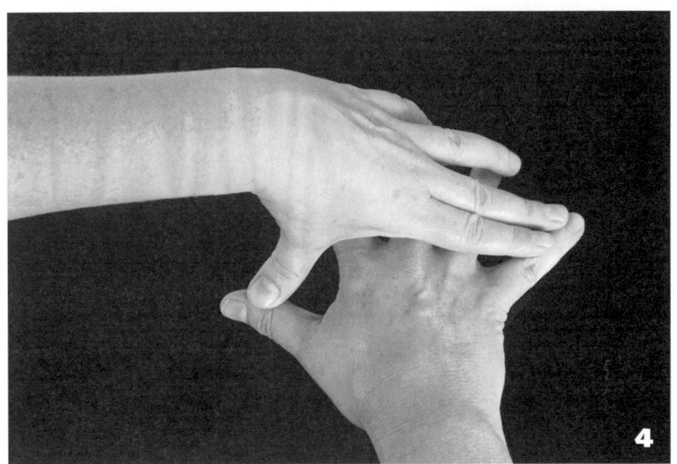

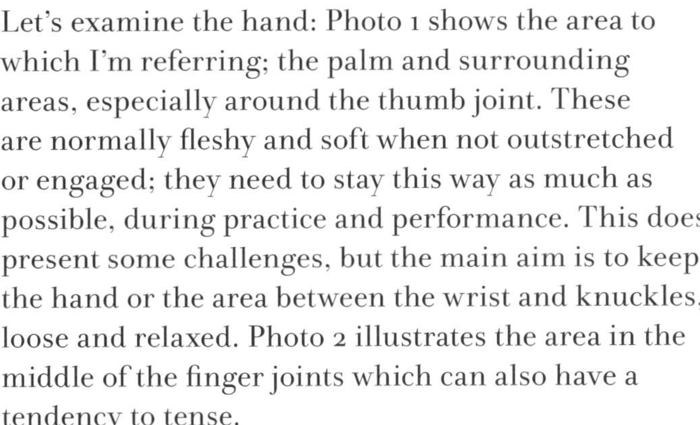

Let's examine the hand: Photo 1 shows the area to which I'm referring; the palm and surrounding areas, especially around the thumb joint. These are normally fleshy and soft when not outstretched or engaged; they need to stay this way as much as possible, during practice and performance. This does present some challenges, but the main aim is to keep the hand or the area between the wrist and knuckles, loose and relaxed. Photo 2 illustrates the area in the middle of the finger joints which can also have a tendency to tense.

Here are a few ideas to loosen the hand, helping it to feel less restricted during practice and performance. First, become aware of how flexible your hand actually is; with your left hand, feel the palm and surrounding fleshy areas of your right hand. Does it feel relaxed and malleable, or tight and locked-up? When relaxed, most hands are pliable, therefore aim for a comfortable, soft 'feeling' as you play. Learn the feeling of looseness and keep referring to this sensation.

Lay your hands on a flat surface away from the keyboard, and determine how far you can open them without detecting any muscle pull or discomfort (see Photo 3).

To begin with it may not be much, but if you practice this exercise, that is, just opening the hand, and keeping it open whilst relaxing or 'letting go' of the muscles (in the hand, wrist and arm) regularly, then your hands will become accustomed to being 'open' or outstretched. They will eventually be able to open out increasingly further whilst still feeling relaxed. Keep in mind the feeling of relaxation in the hand at all times. If you find this awkward, use your other hand to help you keep the hand open as you learn to relax and release or 'let go' of the muscles within (as in Photo 4).

Now play a triad:

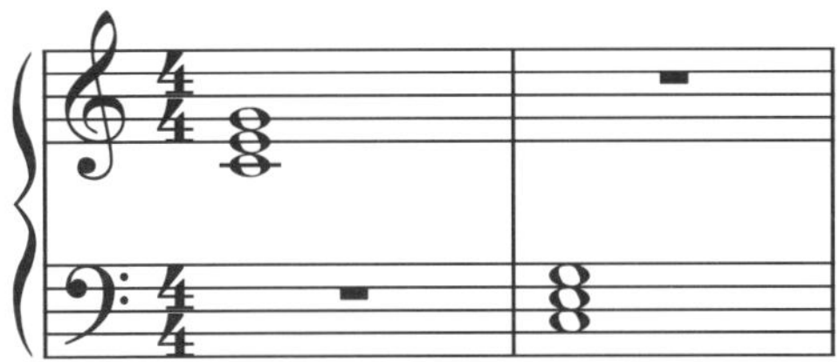

As you play, with your other hand, note how your engaged hand responds whilst playing – are the fleshy areas still relaxed? If they are tense, revert to playing a single note, preferably with the third finger, and as you depress the note, aim to release the muscles within the hand; at first this will require focused concentration. As the note is struck, notice how the muscles react; you must decide if they feel relaxed or tense and uncomfortable. If they are rigid, as the note is held by the finger, relax the surrounding hand by releasing any tension in the wrist and whole arm. Again, you may need to hold the note in place with your other hand until you have learned the sensation of relaxation.

Try this exercise: clench the hand, and then swiftly 'release' the clench, relaxing the muscles. This can be one way of assimilating the feeling of tension and the subsequent 'release' of muscles.

When you feel relaxed playing just the one note, experiment further with the triad in the example, until you can keep the notes depressed without feeling any tightness. Now play two notes a sixth apart, in bars 1 and 3 of the following example:

Rock from side to side as you play this interval (from C to the A and back), 'letting go' of any tension in your hand as you depress the notes. In between the notes, practise dropping your wrist; lowering it in a relaxed manner, as opposed to raising it high above the keyboard. A constantly moving wrist can help tremendously with flexibility; although playing with a low wrist in a fixed position is as inconvenient as playing with one that's too high – my suggestions here are for practice purposes only.

Now play the interval of a sixth (both the C and A) at the same time, as a two-note chord, releasing any tightness in your hand muscles, but still keeping the notes depressed. When this feels comfortable, move up to an interval of a seventh and finally, an octave (as in bars 2 and 4 of the example). As the hand gets used to the wider position, allow your muscles to keep releasing any tension. Eventually the hand will learn to enjoy the outstretched position and its relaxed stance allows for an easier grasp of chords and octaves, fostering a healthier technique, free from pain and discomfort.

Tip

When we learn how to 'let go' of tension as we play, at the same time as keeping the fingers in place, the hand starts to release its grip.

THE BRIDGE POSITION, KNUCKLES AND FINGER STRENGTH

The so-called **Bridge** position is essentially the position the hands assume when the knuckles remain prominent, like this:

5

The Bridge position allows the hand to remain relaxed, yet in control of the fingers, and the fingers in turn can be relatively independent.

In Photo 5, my knuckles remain at the high point of the hand position, clearly visible above each finger, forming a 'bridge' across the hand. The Bridge position wasn't previously mentioned in Book 1 and 2 for the reason that it can prove a distraction for some less experienced players, especially for those in the earlier learning stages. When students slowly develop finger strength gradually and naturally, the Bridge tends to form on its own. This takes time and patience, but by this stage of learning, the Bridge can really benefit piano playing and it is for this reason it is being discussed here.

The Bridge position not only allows the hand to 'balance' properly, but it also forms the basis for strong fingers, particularly the fourth and fifth fingers. This in turn helps with ease of playing octaves, chords and any extended finger pattern.

Without this position, there can be a tendency for the hand to be weighted towards the thumb, second and third finger, whereas when the Bridge has been developed, the third finger can remain at the centre-point of the hand, and the fourth and fifth can potentially be active and strong.

Photo 6 demonstrates a hand position, which can also be practiced away from the keyboard. My fingers are straight, wrists are fairly low and relaxed, and the knuckles protrude. This position is unnatural and should **never** be employed whilst playing, but it will draw your attention to the importance of raised knuckles; if they remain flat or out of sight during piano playing, or are lower than the hand or fingers, then the hand won't feel aligned and using the outer fingers with any strength might prove uncomfortable and cause physical problems. Each knuckle connected to every finger and thumb should ideally be raised, particularly those belonging to the weaker, outer fingers.

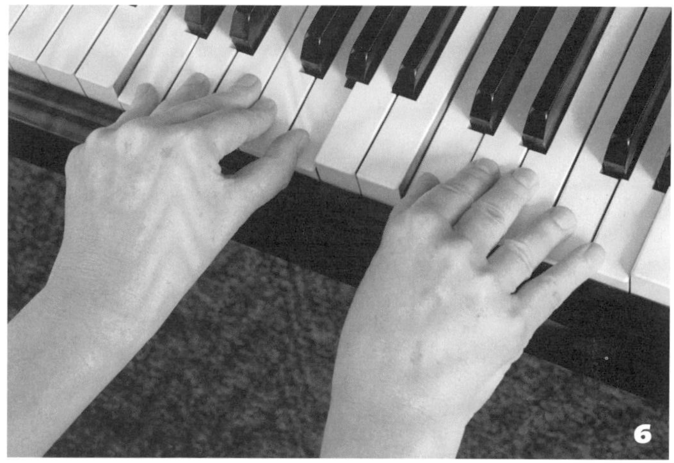
6

The following exercises can be done at the start of a practice session, perhaps after a warm-up, and just for a few minutes; observe your hand positions as you play. Similarly, when working at repertoire, aim to think carefully about the upper body. As mentioned in *Play it again: Piano Book 1* and 2, the whole arm and wrist must feel supple, relaxed and loose. Only the fingers and their corresponding knuckles should be firm.

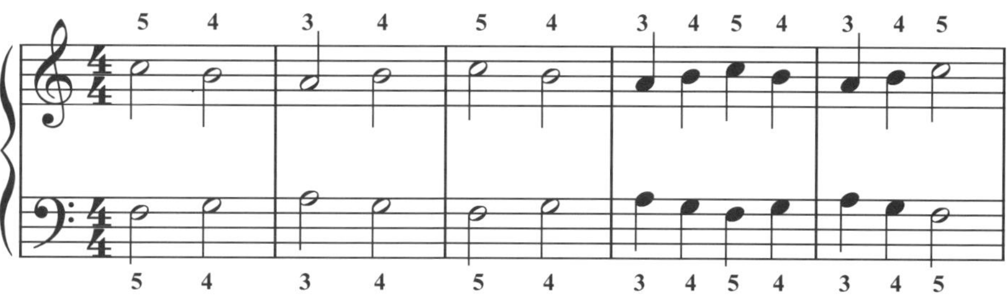

As you depress each note, sink into the keys, down to the key bed, past the double escapement action or the 'jolt' felt at the bottom of the key (on grand pianos) and aim to play on the tips of your fingers, with the finger joints fully engaged. This will require some thought and care when using the outer fingers, and may therefore feel unnatural at first. Between each half note (minim), keep your wrist and arm completely relaxed; it can help to use a circular wrist motion (as discussed in Book 1 and 2). Observe the knuckles as you play, so they don't disappear and they remain firm, that is, they don't sink into the hand.

In the example above, try to balance the hand using the third finger as a pivot, moving the wrist laterally (lateral wrist motion is discussed on page 69) to the right as you play from E to G (as in Photo 7), then back to E as the centre point, moving laterally to the left when playing down to middle C.

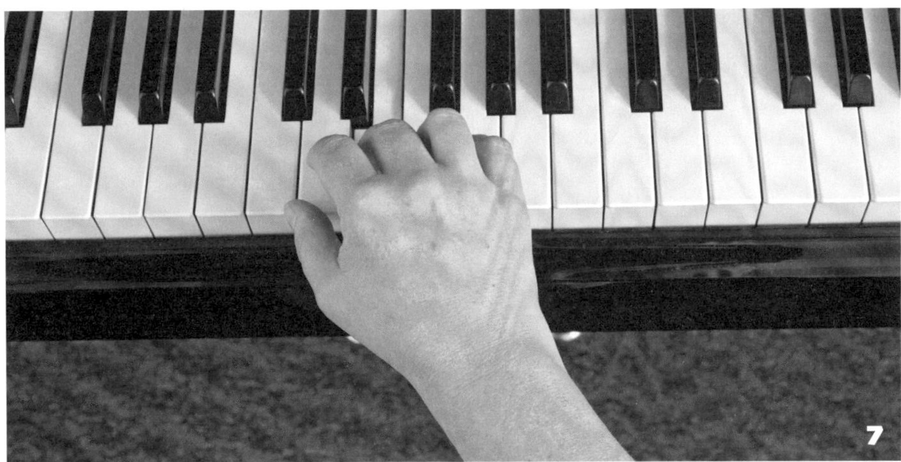
7

These exercises will hopefully help to cultivate finger independence, and will draw your attention to the necessity of fully engaging the weaker fingers (the fourth and fifth). There are many exercises which may prove valuable here by a variety of composers, but irrespective of your choice, practice little and often so that suppleness remains in the upper body and crucially, nothing causes pain.

Tip

If you can observe and correct movements as you practice, after a period of time, they will become a habit – a good habit!

THUMBS

Thumb exercises have been included in Book 2 (see page 9), but now we will take them a step further, focusing on thumb movement and slightly more demanding exercise patterns. It's too easy for the thumb to strike a key, with little direction, or physical or tonal control. The following exercises are designed for thumb movement awareness, building digital control and thumb joint flexibility.

Circular Thumb Patterns:

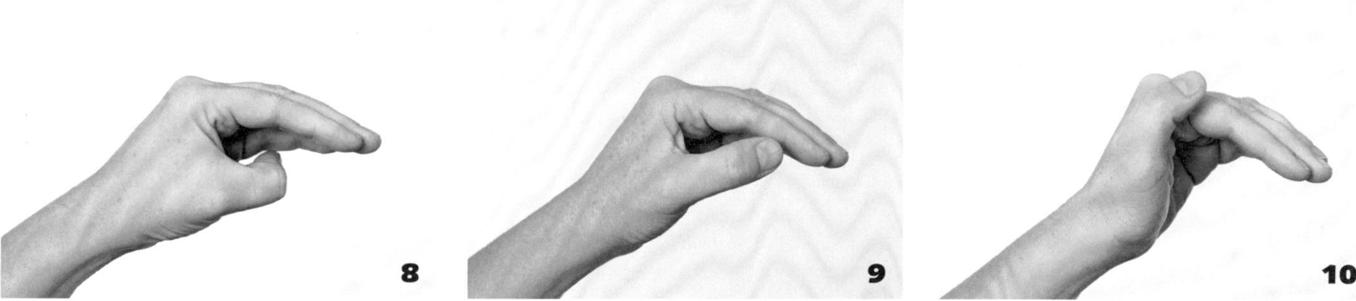

Photo 8 shows the thumb in a lowered position with the thumb under the hand, photo 9 shows the thumb as it passes through the middle position, and photo 10 illustrates the higher position of the thumb. As the thumb passes through these positions, it forms a circular upward movement. Practice moving the large thumb joint at the base of the thumb flexibly between these positions, guiding the thumb up and down; do this slowly, with pliable muscles whilst keeping the rest of the hand still, yet relaxed. The mastery of this movement makes larger intervals using the thumb, such as thumb under movements necessary in scales and arpeggios, that much easier.

Now try the following exercise:

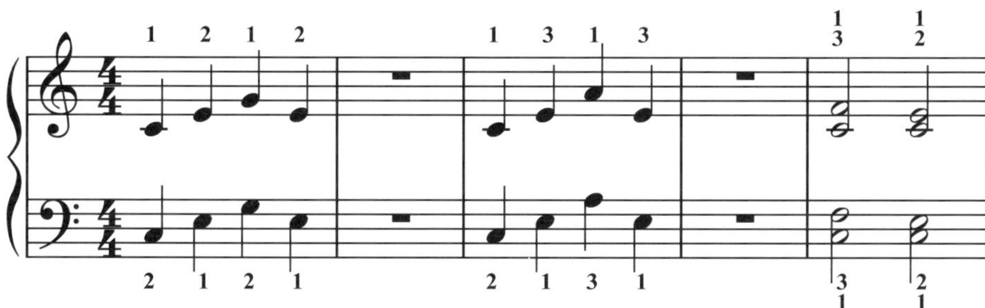

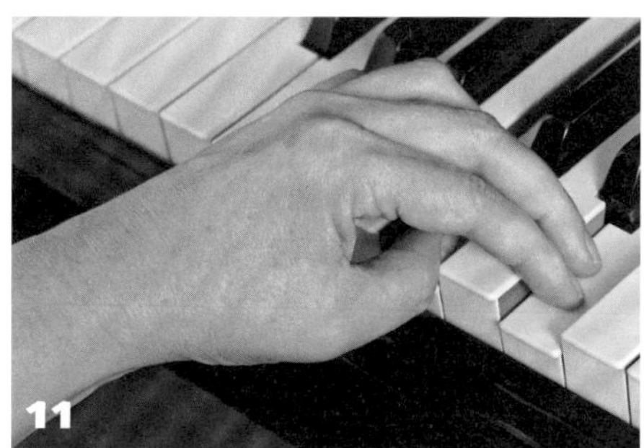

Photo 11 demonstrates the relaxation needed in the hand to play the intervals in bar 5 (of the example above) without feeling tight, taut or tense in any way. Once you can do this easily, that is, you feel completely relaxed and loose whilst keeping the notes depressed, playing larger thumb under movements, such as those found in arpeggios, will feel comfortable and painless and will hopefully lead to note accuracy and smooth *legato* playing.

Exploring the wonderful thumb resonance might also be a helpful exercise. The following example demands a soft thumb approach, using the weight of your arm, essentially exploring sonority. Employ the fleshier area of the thumb tip, that is, the area before the very tip or end of the thumb, and start by playing softly, building the sound throughout the exercise. Allow your thumb to 'keybed', or touch and press notes at the same time, or play to the bottom of the key (there are many descriptions for this activity), past the point in the key bed where we experience a sudden 'jolt' or escapement action.

In this exercise, the thumb movement should ideally be combined with a loose wrist and arm to produce a 'full' or rich sound. The wrist will need to move up and down freely for a full tone; down as each note is depressed, 'cushioning' the thumb as it plays deeply and into the key, and up as the note is released. The sustaining or right pedal might be an enjoyable addition to this exercise to begin with, and aim to change your sound on each individual note:

Now try the following exercise, joining each note with no gaps in the sound. To do this successfully, you will need to listen to the ends of notes; keep the first note depressed right until the end of the beat and then quickly leave it, playing the second carefully to match the sound of this second note to the decay of the first one. It requires a quick, precise movement but a slower key depression; even though some of the intervals are larger here, you can still aim to 'join' the sound.

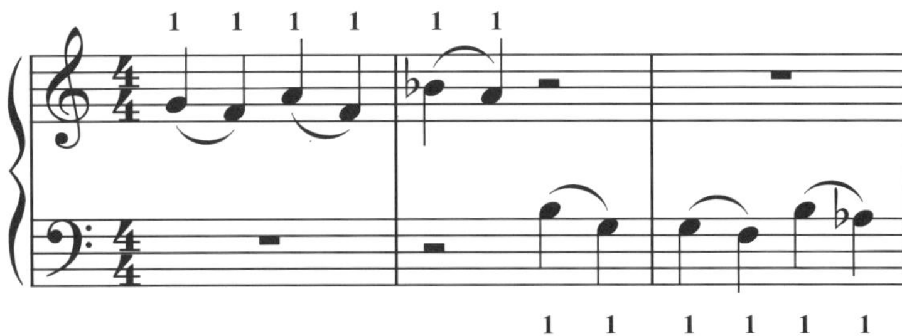

Another interesting exercise for thumb control is the chromatic scale:

Unconventional fingering, such as in the example above, will encourage thumbs to move actively and seek to play each note fully, depressing the key attentively for accuracy. Try replacing the second finger with the third for variety.

Tip

At no point should these movements feel uncomfortable or painful; on the contrary, they are designed to encourage various parts of the hand to move easily, freely and actively.

Post Grade 8 Diploma

Sonata in E major

Domenico Scarlatti (1685–1757)

Set up

Key: E major
Time signature: 3/4
Tempo: Andante ♩ = 80
Style: Baroque
Technical Focus: Ornamentation, articulation, phrasing, and balance of sound between the hands.

Italian composer Scarlatti wrote over 555 sonatas for the harpsichord. Whilst generally short works, they contain some of the most idiomatic writing for the instrument; full of harmonic surprises, technical challenges and melodic expressivity. This Binary form Sonata fully illustrates Scarlatti's style and possesses a simplistic beauty.

PREPARATION

For the scale and arpeggio of E major, please refer to Book 1 (page 107). The opening introduction sets the scene for the whole piece. Improvisatory in character, it might be described as two separate voices answering each other; I like to think of it as an oboe and cor anglais enjoying a conversation!

The opening ornamental patterns might be written out like this:

For smoothness and fluency, think of this opening as one phrase, and ensure the fourth and fifth fingers are working efficiently. This could be practiced as a five finger exercise around E major. Focus on moving the wrist laterally (for lateral wrist motion, visit page 69) guided by a relaxed forearm, to the right or away from the body for the first note group, bar 1, beat 2, and then to the left, bar 1, beat 3, and bar 2, beats 1 and 2, supporting the weaker fingers. The fingers require powerful clarity, producing a rich tone, matching the other fingers, and allowing for crisp, clear articulation.

When practicing each note group, try using the following techniques for bar 1 and all similar passages:

Start with a *fortissimo* dynamic for each note group, playing deeply into the keys, very slowly until you can easily negotiate every note with the suggested fingering; play the note groups evenly and rhythmically listening carefully; you could practice each group in the introduction in this manner. Practice tools such as repetitions, accents, various touches, and dynamic contrasts, will help attain independent finger strength. However, only do this in short bursts.

Ornaments

This sonata features several types of ornament or embellishment (the trill, *appoggiatura*, and *acciaccatura*). Book 2 contains more information about ornaments (page 118). The ornaments here are to be played on the beat. Here are a few practice ideas:

Let's take the trill from bar 3, beat 3, which must be perfectly coordinated in both hands. The trill would usually begin on the upper note in this style, and will essentially be a four note trill. However, as it appears at the end of a phrase, you may prefer to elongate this trill, so that it extends to cover the entire beat. Practice this passage very slowly, with a deep tone at first; playing beyond the double escapement action, giving the second and fourth notes special attention:

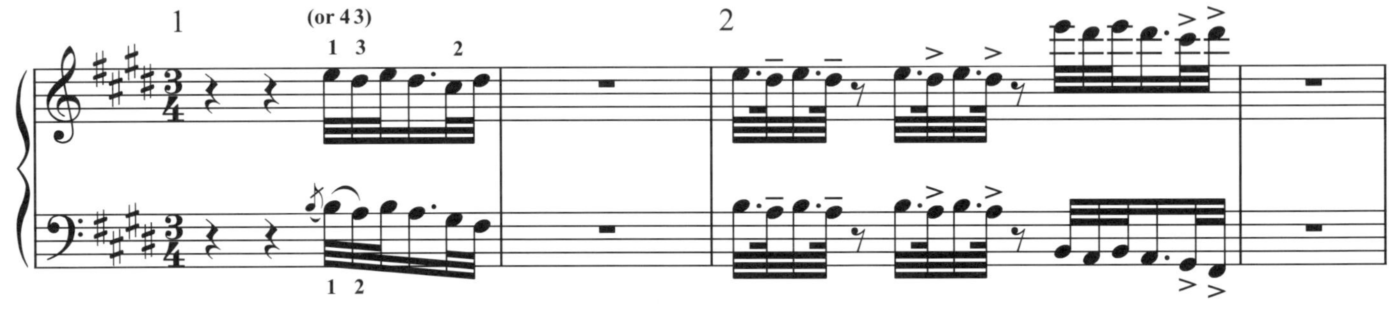

It's easy to 'swallow' or rush these notes; make sure they sound clearly and are equal in length to the first and third notes of the ornament. Applying different rhythmic practice patterns helps to assimilate the feeling of the fingers striking the keys at precisely the same moment, as does practicing in different octaves around the keyboard, as notated in the example. Concentrate on the final note in each trill; this, too, can suffer from rushing or 'tripping over' to the next beat or bar. Now repeat these practice suggestions with accentuation on the first and third notes in the trill.

Listen to all notes in every embellishment pattern; they must sound neat and expertly coordinated with active fingers. For practice purposes, I've included the tied B (first note in the left hand, beat 3) to coincide with the right hand, but you may prefer to practice as written, that is, played before the main beat.

Once you've practiced with a full tone, lighten your touch, keep fingertips close to the keys, and apply minimal finger movement, akin to softly skimming across the keys. After the heavy preparation work, fingers should move easily, producing an even tone, free from bumps. How fast can you play these passages? Experiment at all speeds, from very slow to extremely fast, eventually settling on a manageable speed, suitable for both the passage and your fingers.

Scarlatti gave minimal indication as to the length of his *appoggiaturas*, but it is generally assumed that they take half the time of the original note. Phrase off *appoggiaturas*, such as those at the end of each section (bars 41 and 89), with a much lighter second note, matching the tone evenly:

When articulating ornaments, resist the urge to lock or stiffen the wrist or hand; aim to keep them flexible and relaxed, remembering that the fingers should work from the knuckles, supported by a relaxed hand and wrist.

PRACTICE TECHNIQUES

Right-hand practice

The eighth note (quaver) triplet passages from bars 4–12 form part of an extended introduction, stating the theme. Play them as chords to help find the note shapes and fingerings; some suggested fingering has been added to the score. Although fingers will need to articulate triplets rhythmically and with clean, clear *legato* finger work, that is, picking up each finger avoiding any sound overlay, tied quarter notes (crotchets) are also in the mix. Hold tied notes fully, for example, bar 4, beat 3 to bar 5, beat 1, for the required resonant effect. This is often offset by the harmonic resolution in the left hand, as in bar 5, beat 1. This technique will also be important at bars 14–20, 34–35, 54–61, 69–74 and 82–85.

Aim to colour the top of the melodic material, especially the held quarter notes from bars 4–11 and 54–61, and some tied eighth notes at the end of the bar, such as that at bar 6. At bar 5, the G♯ on beat 2, whilst an eighth note and first beat of a triplet, must lead to the A on beat 3, and beat 1 of bar 6. Balance the sound attentively, so that the melody rings out and the lower notes act almost as an accompaniment.

Melodic expressivity can be achieved by timely nuancing; in bar 14, for example, the ornament on beat 1, which is to be placed on the beat, could be phrased with a leaning or a *tenuto* on the first note (D♮), followed by a slightly deeper touch on the quarter note, F♯. The climax of this two bar phrase, is the quarter note, B (bar 14, beat 3), which must be coloured sufficiently, and it must also be graded and 'placed', so that it lasts for the entire two beats, bars 14, beat 3, and 15, beat 1, soaring above other melodic notes. The phrase might die away on beat 3 of bar 15:

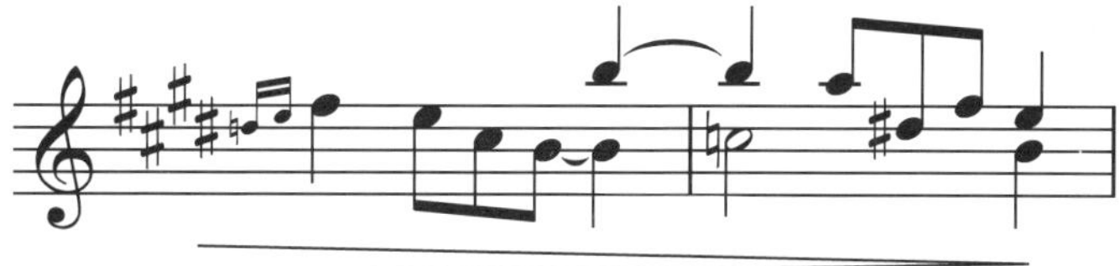

A *cantabile* touch is usually reserved for the Romantic style, and whilst a rich resonance isn't a necessity in this work, the melody must sing out above the accompaniment. Triplet beats should be even and equal. Try sub-dividing the quarter note beat, counting in triplets; you could even set the metronome to a triplet beat. I find it helpful to count each eighth note triplet in six sixteenth notes (semiquavers) too.

Tip

Locate all the ornamental passages and mark them according to dynamic colour, nuance and contextual importance.

Left-hand practice
The left hand plays a vital supporting role. A lighter articulation is preferable, but the bass does provide occasional colour, and harmonic interest, for example at bars 16–21.

A *legato* touch for notes moving by step works well, and for those moving by interval, *non-legato*. This might help as a starting point for interpretation. Left hand octave F♯s in bar 40 (on beats 2 and 3) before the double bar, can be lightly detached, but the preceding step-wise notes, smooth, providing a welcome contrast from the right hand 'sighs'.

Non-legato is most effective when (for quarter and half notes (minims)) the note is held almost to the end of the beat, lifting the finger cleanly just before playing the next note, leaving a slight gap in the sound. This works well for slow, expressive Baroque works. Keep in mind that the tone of any note should ideally match that of the next.

Chromatic notes and chords will benefit from a deeper touch combined with a miniscule amount of time taken in order to 'place' them, so as to make the listener aware of their importance; for example, at bar 39, beat 2, an A♯.

At bars 29–31 and 75–77, the downward bass pattern must lead the right hand, with a *crescendo* to the D♯ at bar 32 (beat 1) and E, at bar 78 (beat 1). Similarly, the left hand assumes a major role in bar 37–41 and 85–89, leading the right hand's melodic whimpers.

Tip

A *portato* articulation means 'to carry' and is akin to a smooth, pulsating articulation of a note or notes.

A *portato* with added *tenuto* touch might be beneficial for passages such as bars 4–13 and 54–63. Add such articulation to the first beat of each bar to give rhythmic shape and melodic assistance to the melody.

Fermata, pauses and breathing space

The term *fermata* originated from the word *fermare*, meaning to stay or stop. The *fermata* means a pause or a pause sign, as in bar 13. Creating breathing space in this work is paramount.

The beginning of bar 4 is the end of the introduction; ensure a slight break, lifting the fingers off the keys before playing beat 2. Punctuating each phrase in this way allows the work to breath and gives the listener time to register the difference between musical sections.

At bars 13 and 63, a pause has been written in the score after arpeggio figurations, on the last note of the phrase, implying a lengthening of this note; an F♯ at bar 13 and a B at bar 63. Historically, pauses also imply a slowing down, and this might be effective here, especially if you momentarily dwell on the A♯ in bar 12, prior to the F♯.

From bars 14 to 29, phrases are short, often just two bars in length, and a small breathing space from one phrase to the next feels natural and allows each phrase to build intensity. Consider similar articulation from bars 15 to 16, bar 22 (before beat 2), and bar 24, (before beat 2). The same occurs from bars 64–68. Other important breathing points; bars 45, 49, and 53 (at the end of each four bar phrase).

Pausing for harmonic effect might be considered at the start of bars 34 and 87. Such breaks will be small, probably just a millisecond or two, but make all the difference in a considered interpretation.

Hands together
The balance between hands is crucial; the bass line will generally need a softer tone, whilst the melodic material can be bolder and brighter.

One of the most interesting parts of this work is from bars 42–53. Here, Scarlatti employs breathtakingly chromatic harmonies. Three bar repetition is a Scarlatti trademark providing emphasis, and each phrase or four bars must build on the last in tonal and dramatic quality. Define each chord, even using an accent for definition, and they could also be spread (as played on the harpsichord), resembling the strumming of a guitar (bars 42–44):

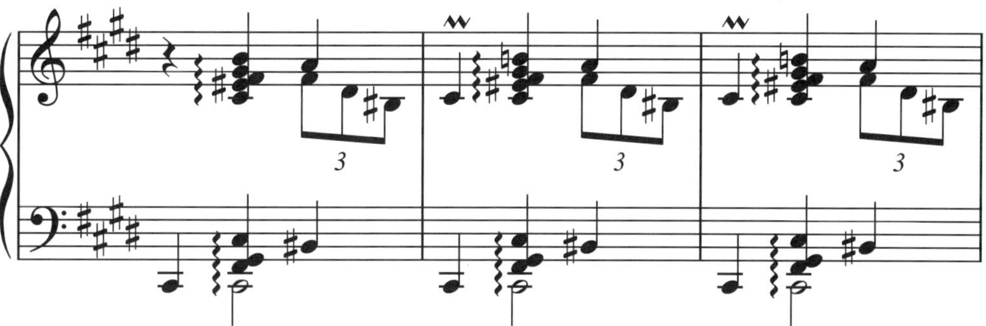

The first bass note, on beat 1 of each bar, requires accentuation and the third beat of the bar can be softer. Scarlatti moves from four sharps to four flats, building further tension, and this mood must be continued until bar 54, where a familiar note pattern recurs.

Practice will be needed to become accustomed to a *non-legato* bass line combined with a mostly *legato* melody.

INTERPRETATION

Tempo should remain the same throughout, with the possible exception of the opening four bars. *Rubato* (or taking time) will require thoughtful balance; it might be judicious at the ends of phrases or to add extra nuance. A work such as this would be dry without use of the sustaining pedal. However, this must be employed carefully, to provide resonance at the ends of phrases and depth in chordal passages. Some suggested pedalling has been added.

As often the case in Scarlatti's sonatas, the chromaticisms (or added chromatic notes) add a rich expressive quality, and with this in mind, aim to use them to help form a musically satisfying interpretation.

Sonata in E major

K. 215

Domenico Scarlatti (1685–1757)

Ped.
p

Wedding Day at Troldhaugen

Edvard Grieg (1843–1907)

Hailing from the eighth volume of Lyric Pieces, Wedding Day at Troldhaugen *has remained a firm favourite in the repertoire. Set in Ternary form, it displays many hallmarks of the composer's style, and exudes a joy and tenderness.*

Set up

Key: D major
Time signature: C
Tempo: *Tempo di marcia un poco vivace:* ♩ = 132, and *Poco tranquillo:* ♩ = 76
Style: Romantic
Technical Focus: Melodic articulation and part playing, large chords, rapid passagework split between the hands, and *cantabile.*

PREPARATION

For the scale and arpeggio of D major, please revisit Book 1 (page 36). The outer sections are sprightly, forthright and dramatic; perhaps indicative of wedding preparations. One of the challenges is to combine a powerful sonority punctuated with clear articulation and dynamic variation, yet free of a harsh or forced tone.

The following exercise might be useful to develop a powerful sound, which will be necessary from bars 40–56 and 146–162.

Start by assimilating the chordal shapes; let's look at bar 45. If we take the A♭ major chord in isolation (1 in the example), we can focus on sound quality alone. Keeping your upper body very relaxed and loose, play the chords in the example below (1). Silently prepare each note of the chord by touching, or resting the finger on the key in advance, then slowly depress each key at the same time using the arm as a hinge coupled with a soft, relaxed wrist, moving in a downward motion. Come up to play the next chord without your fingers leaving the key surface, that is, your wrist and arm shouldering most of the movement. This is basic arm-weight:

Balance your hand and fingers, so that the notes of each chord sound altogether, that is, the notes are played at the same time and not split. Work at this thoroughly, experimenting with the balance required. In Exercise 2, the fifth finger might need extra weight from the arm, to depress the key evenly and at the same moment as the other fingers. The accent on the A♭ and arrow marking serve as reminders to balance the hand towards the top, so that it can provide melodic interest.

Once you can do this, play the following chords with the suggested dynamics, also adding a chord in the bass.

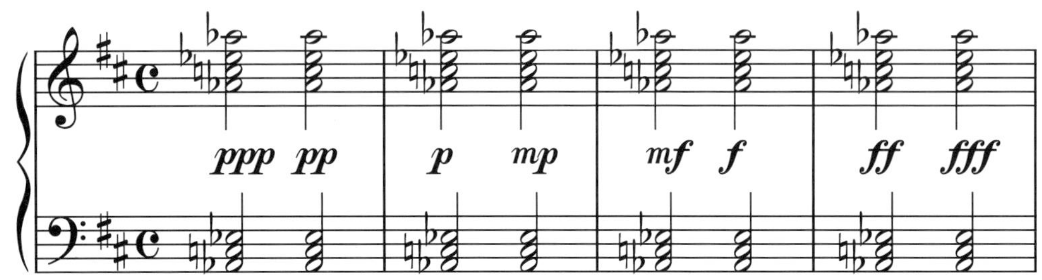

As the chords become increasingly powerful, aim to use your wrist as a hinge, allowing your arm to move optimally providing the necessary weight behind every note; you can practice varied amounts of leverage, starting from a *pianissimo* going to a *fortissimo.* As you strike a chord, the wrist should ideally 'cushion' the sound, moving downwards with an almost circular motion, as you go to play or sound the notes. This will avoid a harsh tone, allowing the arm and shoulder to help unleash the piano's full timbre. The climaxes will all benefit from this technique. It can help to think of the fingers as an extension of the arm when applying arm-weight.

PRACTICE TECHNIQUES

Right-hand practice

The main theme has been carefully articulated. Start by working at each musical line separately, lifting off after *staccato* notes, but not too much; aim for *non-legato* or a light inward 'scratching' or flicking movement with the top of the fingers.

Weight the top line by moving your hand and wrist slightly to the right, away from the body, supporting the fingers whilst keeping them firm but wrists, relaxed.

After each short phrase, break any tension in your hand and wrist by allowing a minuscule gap; for example, after the quarter note (crotchet) at bar 4, between beats 3 and 4. Here, you can consciously free muscles and tendons, which also offers a breathing space between phrases.

The sixteenth note (semiquaver) triplet at the beginning of the theme (bar 2, beat 4), can be practiced with a deeper touch; make sure the second and third notes of the triplet are not rushed. Articulate them precisely; you could count all three notes aloud to ta-te-ta – or similar, ensuring they are even and accurately placed. Ornaments, at bars 26 and 31 (both on beat 1), might require similar practice, so they are not 'lost' in the texture.

When each musical line is secure and, if possible, memorised, play them together, keeping the lower line light, with a relaxed thumb. To accent powerful chords in the climaxes (at bar 49, for example), use a quick upward movement, after the second eighth note (quaver) of beat 2, followed by a downward motion with your wrist at the moment of impact, for example, in bar 49 with a break between beats 2 and 3. This helps to alleviate any tension in the hand and wrist, and punctuates the music.

If you have a smaller hand, you could leave notes out of the larger chords, but you can also work at playing these with confidence by using the hand exercises in the technique section at the beginning of this book. The following chord comes from bar 48, beats 3 and 4:

After you've relaxed the hand in the open position, rock the note pattern, from side to side, drop your wrist whilst holding notes in place, and relax the whole hand (1). Now play the notes together (2). As you play the octaves, be aware of the necessary flexible feeling in your hand.

Add any inner notes in the chords (3), carefully extending your fingers onto the correct notes. Do this exercise little and often, avoiding any pain and tension. Finally, you may eventually feel comfortable reaching the large chord (4 of the example) with guided, relaxed practice.

To practice the large chord (4), start by focusing on the inner notes, the G, A and C♯ (played by the thumb and second finger), producing a full sound, whilst keeping the outer notes (played by the fourth and fifth finger), light. Now reverse this, and play the outer notes, played by the fourth and fifth finger, with a full sound, keeping the inner parts soft. This dynamic reversal encourages concentration of different notes within the chord, allowing for a more even hand and finger balance. Eventually the chord should feel easier to play, and balance won't be such as issue.

Left-hand practice

The left hand requires power in the climaxes. Assimilate note patterns and pay attention to fingering, especially in passages such as bars 49–56; these need to be assured before hands are played together. When negotiating the rapid chord passages, from bar 35, beat 4, to bar 39, beat 3, lateral wrist movement will be useful as the intervals become larger and move over the octave (in bar 39, beats 1–3). See page 69 for information on lateral wrist motion.

If the chords at bars 39, beat 4 to bar 41, beat 3 are too large to handle, omit the top note (F♮). It's not necessary for the octaves to be *fortissimo* throughout; you can shape them efficiently, with rhythmic clarity and crisp articulation. Begin by practicing using a deep touch, slowly with a relaxed open hand. It can help to guide the octave with the thumb, then the fifth finger. Work separately at first, adding accents and varied touches to develop confident keyboard geography (bar 41–43):

Find the shape of each note group, so you can move cleanly and decisively. When up to speed, lighten your touch, accenting on the first and third beat of each group. This should encourage swift, lighter movement.

Hands together

The opening fifths need a percussive sound. Observe accents and give the final quarter note of each three-note group its full value, as opposed to a short sharp *staccato* articulation.

Practice a beat at a time very slowly at first, leaving as much as two seconds between each sixteenth-note beat; this offers enough time to grasp the necessary movements.

Rhythmic precision might feel challenging in bars such as 49, where the right-hand chordal melody is accompanied by groups of five or six (as at bar 51) sixteenth notes. Aim to know the note patterns and rhythms so that they are embedded in your fingers and mind.

Rhythm Tapping

Let's tap the rhythm at bar 49, beats 2 and 3, on the top of the keyboard:

It can help to place the third note of the quintuplet with the second eighth (quaver) note; therefore two sixteenths are placed with the first eighth note (see 1 in the rhythmic example), and three with the second. Now reverse this, so you are playing eighth notes with your left hand:

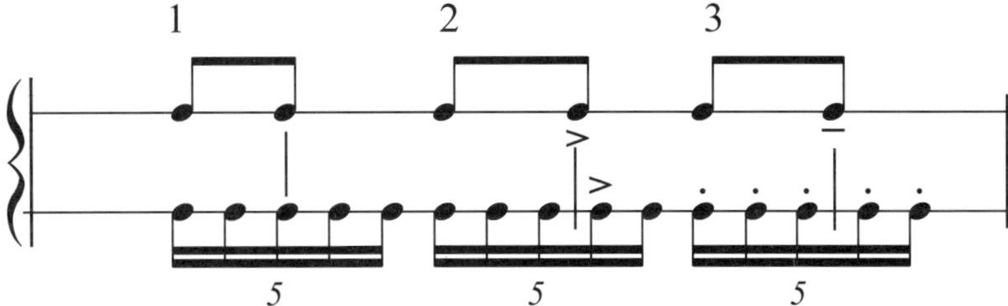

Finally, experiment with 2 and 3 in the example, placing the second eighth note between the third and fourth sixteenth note. Once secure, transfer to the piano and relax the rhythm a little. Slow practice is key, and accents can help too. As speed is added, this pattern should feel more natural.

Shifting positions rapidly is a feature. Moving between chords at bars 45–48, keep fingers in position, so they are aware of the chord shape, and when practicing, extend the pattern to cover the entire keyboard; this will cement the large movements. Swift changes will allow for sound preparation and accuracy; aim to arrive at each chord slightly before the beat, preparing your fingers on the keys in advance, and think of the pattern in each bar as a chordal sweep, flowing from the bottom to the top of the keyboard.

The completely contrasted middle section, in a new key (G major) and in 2/4, appears serenely tranquil after the drama of the beginning. This might allude to the wedding ceremony or possibly the tenderness between the lovers. A gentle *cantabile* touch will suffice for the melodic material, which is passed from treble to bass, as though a conversation between the bride and groom. Try to match the sound between notes in the melody line, whilst the accompanying material remains light. It's a question of balancing the layers of texture. Some passages can be passed between the hands to create *legato*; as in bar 60, where the right hand can strike the B (beat 1), which forms the first note of the left hand's answering phrase.

Split Passagework

A large portion of this work places rapid left-hand figurations against the right. This might be known as 'split' or broken passagework. To learn this efficiently, block out the following chords which are from bar 31, beat 4 and bar 32:

In order to feel the rhythmic pulse here, try the following four practice suggestions:

When finally reverting to the written score, heavily accent the first and third beats of each note group, eventually reducing the accents to the first beat only. Avoid rushing and keep inner parts light.

The right-hand's top line must sing out with the melody, therefore weight your hand towards the weaker fingers. Play the line alone with the intended fingering; use a deep touch, so that when the lower parts are added, the melody is still to the fore. A lateral motion will be imperative in the left hand.

Try to ensure that the lower notes in each split chord in the left hand are given a full sonority. They are those on the off-beat and are usually played with the fifth finger (the lower E♭ in the above examples). If they are given more weight and a sense of being 'placed', there will be less temptation to 'rush' each note, therefore keeping the pulse steady throughout.

Aim to keep the hands, wrists and arms loose and relaxed when playing this passagework; you can do this by releasing tension after every two bar phrase, when it's necessary to change note patterns, such as between bar 35, beats 3 and 4.

Illusion of legato

Melody notes can't always be joined for a smooth *legato*. Occasionally, it's necessary to create the 'illusion' of *legato*:

Join the right-hand passage in the example above using fourth and fifth fingers only, very smoothly. Listen to the ends of each note, moving the finger off the first note at the last moment, manoeuvring your finger onto the next note as quietly and effortlessly as possible, so that there is no gap in the sound and the tone of the second note matches that of the dying first note. Now apply this technique to the first four bars of the middle section:

Once grasped, practice the *poco tranquillo* using this method.

Pedalling has been suggested, and its presence will contribute resonance and depth, particularly in the slower middle section. Depress the sustaining pedal a fraction before the first beat at bars 72 and 104, 'catching' the left hand bass harmonies.

Flutter pedalling will assist in reducing any smudging or blurring of the harmonies as marked by the wavy line beneath the stave at bars 76–79. When 'fluttering' the foot up and down (or hovering) over the Sustaining pedal, keep foot noise to a minimum, and use a shallow foot movement, that is, not depressing the pedal fully, but rather using half of the possible depression. For more information on Partial Pedal Changing and Flutter, see page 148.

A dramatic finish might be more effective with one pedal marking over the entire last line, from bars 174–178. Observe the *una corda* and *tre corde* (directions to depress and lift the left pedal) where marked.

Tip

Grieg makes pointed use of the G major seventh chord throughout, in the outer sections especially; at bar 8, beat 1, for example, adding a rich vibrancy to the texture. Aim to colour these chords with a brighter touch and ringing resonance.

Wedding Day at Troldhaugen

Op. 65 No. 6

Edvard Grieg (1843–1907)

17
20
f
23
LH
dim.
pp dolce
una corda
26
f
tre corde
LH
29
dim.
pp
una corda
pp sempre

32
34
cresc.
tre corde
36
poco a poco
38
più cresc.
(or 1 5)
40
f
5 (or 1 5)

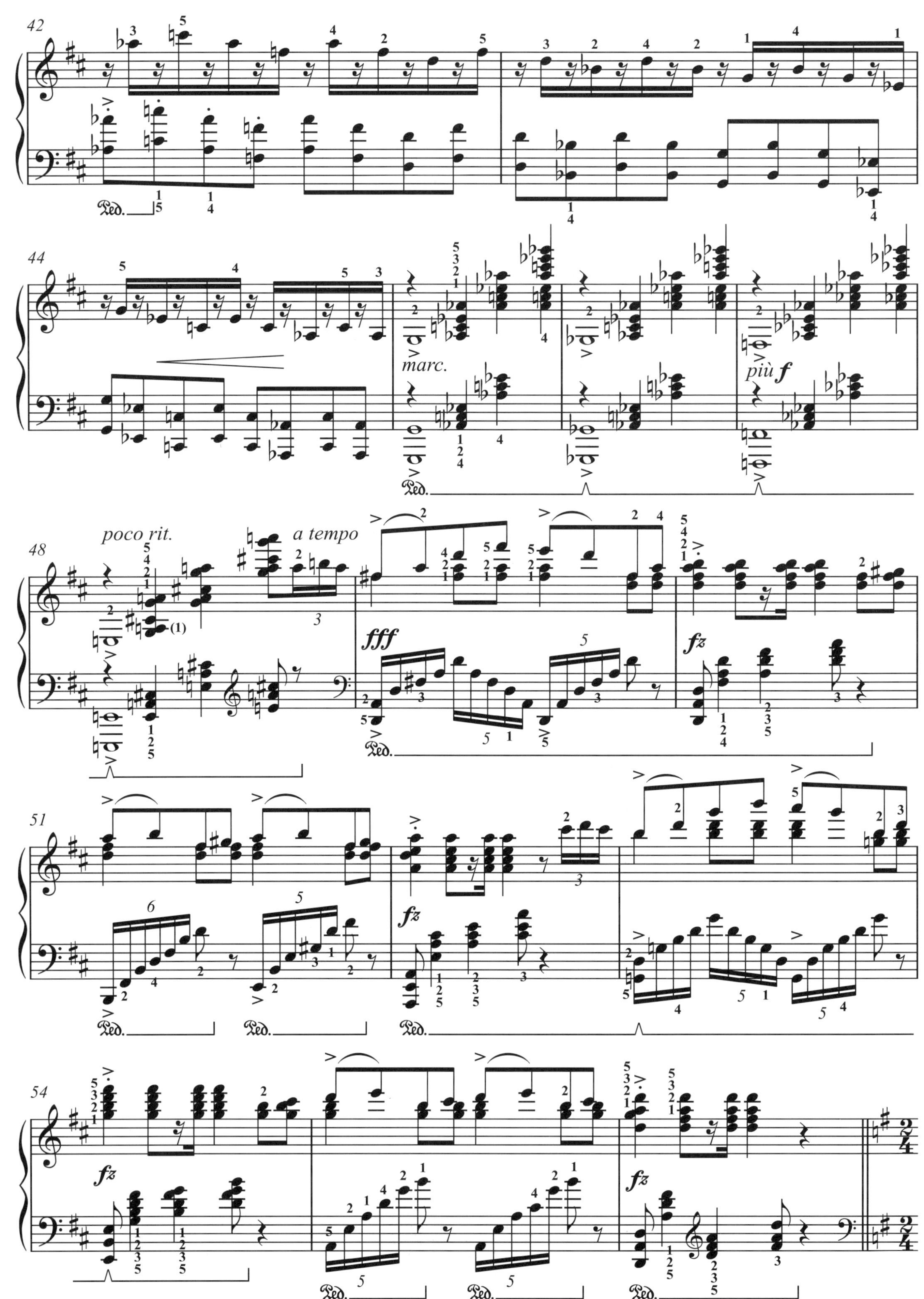

poco rit.
a tempo
marc.
più f
fff
fz

Poco tranquillo ♩ = 76
cantando
p
cantando
sim.
f
3
dolce
pp
dolce
pp
simile

Tempo I

115
pp
119
122
sempre
pp
125
f
129
dim.
pp dolce
una corda
132
f
tre corde

135
dim.
pp
dolce
pp sempre
138
140
cresc.
142
poco a poco
144
più cresc.
146
f

148
150
marcato
più f
poco rit.
a tempo
154
fff
157
160
fff sempre

163
p
staccato sempre
166
p
168
170
dim.
174
sopra
pp
ppp
fffz
Ped.

La puerta del Vino

Claude Debussy (1862–1918)

Set up

Key: D♭ major
Time signature: $\frac{2}{4}$
Tempo: Mouvement de Habanera: ♩ = 63
Style: French Impressionist
Technical Focus: Polyrhythms, double notes, chords, *fioritura* and colour.

The 'Wine Gate' depicts the ancient Moorish entrance at the Alhambra Palace in Granada, Spain. Exotic harmonies, colourful ornamental passages and a hypnotic left hand embodies Flamenco-style singing, the strumming of Spanish guitar, and the dramatic habanera. This seductive dance offers an intriguing juxtaposition of passion and brutality.

PREPARATION

For the key of D♭ major, return to Book 2, page 95. Whilst D♭ major might be the key, the tonality is ambiguous; chromatic inflections abound, particularly in the ornamental passages, which offer both Arabic and gypsy flavours.

POLYRHYTHMS

The following exercise supports the skill of playing duplets against triplets. Some might be confident with this already, but to play the many passages in this work with the necessary precision, this must be assured.

There are two challenging rhythms; the first consists of a triplet against a duplet (as seen here in bar 46, beat 2, example 1), and the second is the triplet against the dotted duplet (as in bar 17, beat 1, example 2):

1.

2.

Ensure the six (sixteenth note or semiquaver) beats are very rhythmic and equal:

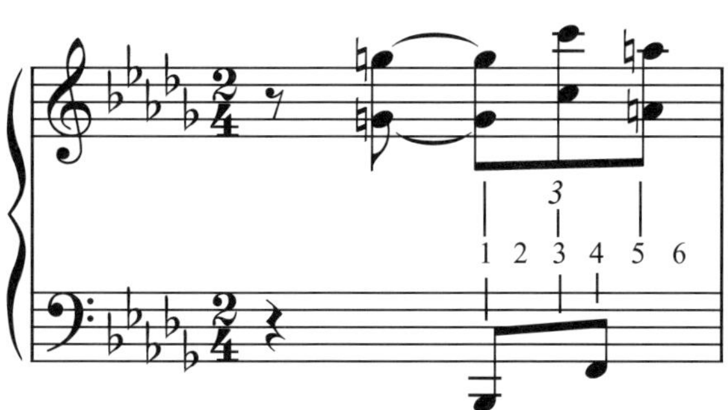

Now try this for the dotted duplet rhythm:

The following practice suggestions may also be helpful; number 1 is the original. Examples 4 and 5 will help to avoid rushing the second left-hand eighth (quaver) note (bar 46, beat 2).

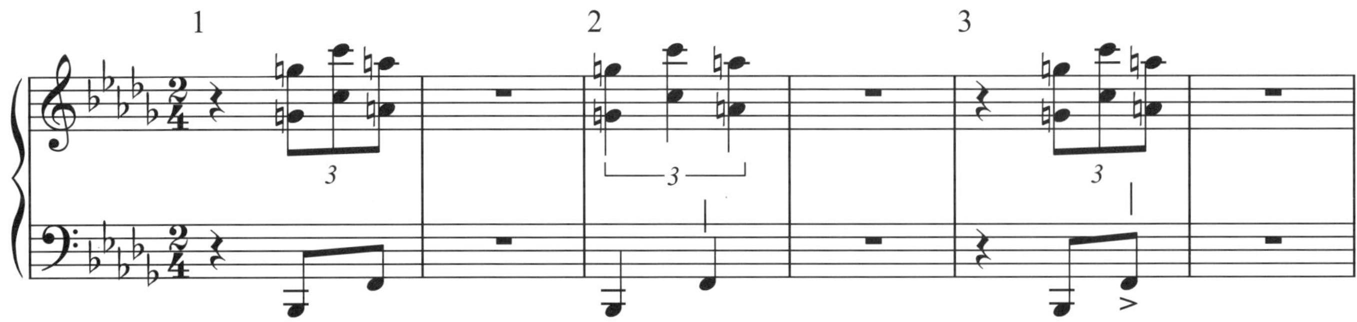

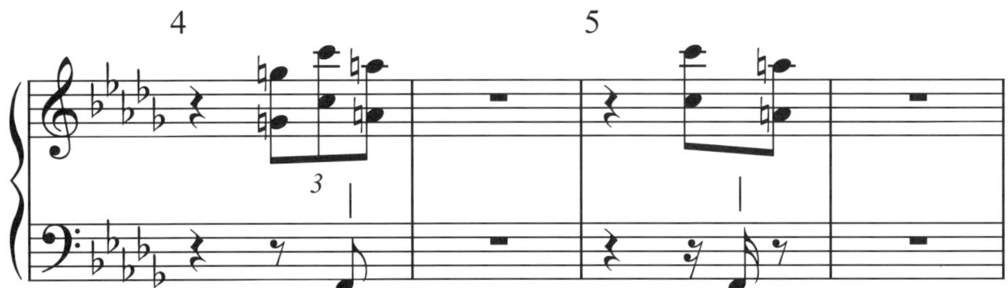

Aim to practice the whole piece rhythmically, then you can relax the tempo adding *rubato* during performance.

Thorough separate hand preparation is required for the complex textures which are often featured over three staves. Some fingering has been added, but this may not suit, and you might want to supplement your own, depending on the size of your hand.

PRACTICE TECHNIQUES

Right-hand practice

Begin by assimilating note patterns. It might be beneficial to learn these first, not adhering to any rhythmic pulse, but rather perfecting the motions needed to move from one part of the keyboard to another. For example, at bar 17, the right hand must jump down to the bass clef. Constant shifting needs attention and a quick, light arm movement.

When learning the following melodic line (which is the theme of this piece), set a very slow pulse. It will be helpful to learn each line separately. Start with the opening melody, without accompaniment (bars 5–12):

Now work at the lower right-hand accompaniment. After separate work, combine the parts. The right hand frequently consists of two-parts; the lower line may need much practice in order to be suitably light and soft, yet articulated. Pay attention to the nuances within the melody; *tenuto* markings and *crescendo/decrescendo* marks within the space of a bar add vital colour.

Fioritura

Fioritura (Italian for 'flourish' or 'flowering') is a feature, and is essentially florid embellishments of the melodic line. Such figurations form an integral part of this work, imitating the Flamenco style singing and guitar strumming. Many note patterns are centred around a single chord, therefore begin practice by playing the notes of the chord altogether. For illustration, let's use the figuration at bar 13 (beat 1):

Once you are sure of the fingering, let's practice this melodic line, with the aim of developing firmer fingers, particularly the fifth:

Work at this example slowly, with much emphasis on each finger, but especially the fifth; only do this for a very short time, so as to not tire the fingers, hand or wrist. Use your fingertips for effective, clear articulation. As marked by the arrows (in bar 1), turn the hand and wrist slightly to the right when playing the outer fingers, and use a rotational or circular wrist motion up to the top B♮; wrist rolling to the right, then away from the B♮, wrist moving to the left. A rhythmical approach will be necessary here therefore try counting every note (at slow speeds). Different touches can be useful when developing finger strength.

When you feel satisfied, gradually increase the tempo and employ a lighter touch.

Chords and octaves in the melody line become more prominent. Practice the outer parts alone, using a deep touch for the tune. Leaps such as the following might require careful preparation (bar 35):

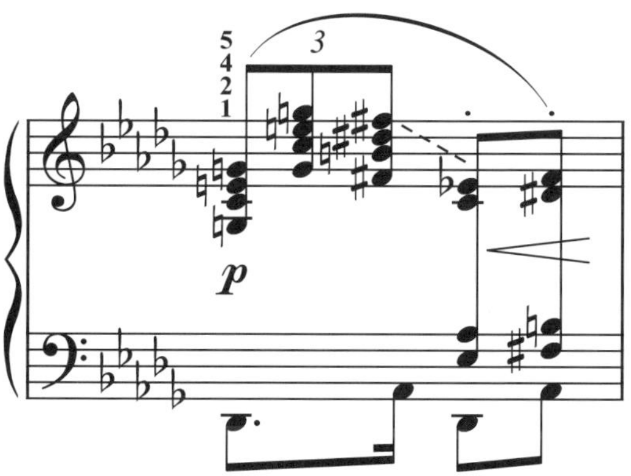

Work at a quarter of the intended speed. During practice, use a wave-like floating lateral forearm rotation, or circular movement, with the wrist shifting extremely quickly, allowing the fingers to skim across the keys. Try to integrate the movements, so that they feel connected. Work at this passage (bar 35, beat 1, first two eighth notes of the triplet) with much larger extensions:

Move swiftly, so you land on the keys before the beat, allowing sufficient time to prepare the sound. When you return to the written passage, the notes should feel more comfortable. It can be useful to be able to 'feel' the jumps without looking, so you can focus on the sound and musical content. It can also help to 'voice' different notes within the chord too, particularly the top note.

Double Notes

Playing several musical lines or two notes together can prove challenging. Let's examine the following double-note passage from bar 74 (beat 1):

Here are some practice suggestions:

1 Hand flexibility exercises, as suggested at the beginning of this book, will be paramount. Keeping the hand soft and flexible, play the top line of bar 74 (bar 1 in the example), then the bottom line (bar 3, in the example):

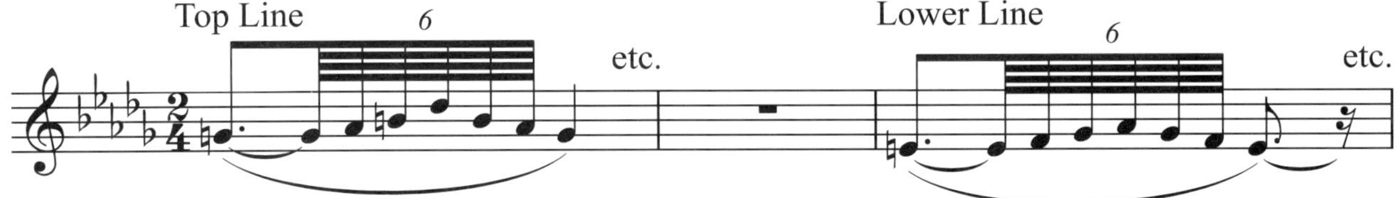

Only use the fingering you intend to use when playing both lines together. Practice softly, and then with firmer fingers accenting every note, using *non-legato* and *staccato* touches.

2 Know each part separately, with no muscular reference to the other part; use the arm as support behind the fingers (arm-weight). Double notes require strong fingers, guided by a light arm and easily moveable elbow; sometimes the arm will need to make little adjustments, so suppleness is key.

3 A flexible wrist employing lateral movement will aid both parts.

4 When playing together, start with the top line, 'marking' the other line by placing the fingers on the notes but not allowing them to sound, then reverse.

5 Play both lines, one soft (*piano*) and the other loud (*forte*), then vice versa. Do the same with different touches; one part *staccato*, the other *non-legato* or *legato* etc.

6 Playing repeated notes can also help; repeating the same note in sixteenth (semiquaver) duplet or triplet patterns (as seen in the Practicing Ornaments section on page 71 of Book 2). You should ideally keep your wrist and arm relaxed, to avoid locking-up. Remember to turn your wrist slightly to the right when focusing on the top line, and to the left, for the lower line.

7 Aim to practice playing broken intervals; this is sometimes known as overlapping intervals (bar 74):

8 When you return to the written passage, you should find you have greater control. Coordination must be exact. Depress each note at the same moment. I would practice slowly, using a heavy touch, in short bursts.

9 When played up to speed, a light, skimming motion will be crucial, the fingers merely grazing over the keys, so they are well coordinated, but sound 'easy' and relaxed.

Left-hand practice

Dominated by the habanera rhythm, a firm rhythmic grasp will be necessary alongside quick alternating chordal accompaniment and nimble ornamental passagework. The habanera pulse may be kept by assiduous counting, with special consideration to the dotted sixteenth note:

Placing the dotted note on the count of four (sixteenth notes) until secure might be the best option; this will be especially important when leaps are involved. Melodic material will benefit from stronger colour, as at bar 58:

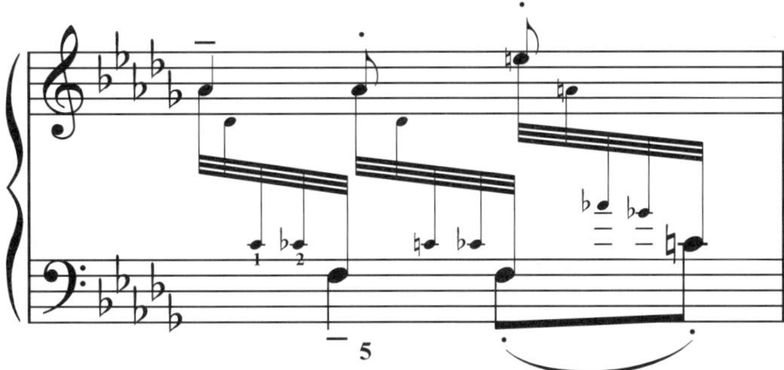

Work at the melody first then add the ornamental passages so they are soft but even.

Hands together

Shifting or changing fingers on the same note is a regular occurrence in order to join the melodic material. For more information on finger substitution, see page 111.

Ornamental passagework will be the main consideration when putting hands together. Play the entire piece without any embellishments; this will help to provide a clear understanding of the outer harmonic and rhythmic structure. Taking the opening four bars, which contain a repeated pattern, let's work at the hands together:

Use the same touch for the ornaments as for the melodic material; deep and heavy, employing the fingertips fully. The practice suggestions, in the example above, will help to create a smooth yet powerful melodic line. If possible, play each ornament on the beat for iridescent tonal sonority. The *acciaccaturas* provide vibrant colour, form part of the character, and often, they are an intrinsic part of the melodic material, therefore they must be played with panache and vigour.

CHORDAL FLOURISHES

A colourful addition to this piece, the chordal flourishes are surely indicative of the Spanish guitar. The following practice suggestions may be useful (based on bar 21):

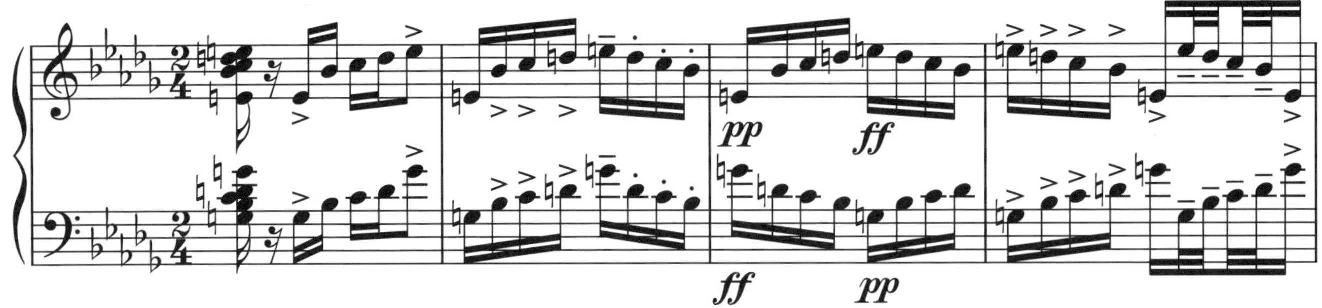

As before, use a heavy touch at first, and as the chords are 'spread', each note must lead onto the next in a rhythmical fashion; accenting will help with coordination, ensemble, and articulation. Every note must be audible, yet the overall effect should be dramatic and dynamic. This applies whether playing *fortissimo* or *pianissimo* passages. Aim to play these figurations on the beat.

CONTRARY MOTION

Note patterns often move in contrary motion. Isolate the necessary sections and practice extending note patterns (1 in the example), working at the outer parts (2), then the inner parts (3), and using your sense of touch to 'feel' the position changes, therefore practicing without looking (bar 46):

Try to secure the note patterns before adding the pulse, and always use the fingering intended for when playing all parts together.

Tip

Pedalling is an integral part of this work. Some has been marked in the score, but you may want to change the markings or add your own. Listening will prove imperative; make good use of flutter or surface pedalling, that is, rapidly and lightly moving the foot up and down when playing the sustaining pedal to clear accumulating sound. Flutter pedal markings have been added too (as at bar 11), and in this style, constantly releasing the sound will determine the success of a performance.

INTERPRETATION

Perhaps the most important element in Debussy's music is the ability to capture vivid tonal colour and create a particular sound world. The subtitle directs the performer beautifully: *avec de brusques oppositions d'extrème violence et de passionnée douceur* or *with sudden opposition of extreme violence and passionate sweetness*. Therefore tonal contrasts are crucial, but can be tricky to implement at speed. Changes can occur within the space of a beat, therefore practice in a similar way to working at leaps; moving quickly, landing on the keys quicker than needed, so you are able to prepare for the sudden variation in the touch and sound, before depressing the keys. The *sforzando* and *forte/fortissimo* markings will benefit from this approach.

Chromatic movement and inflections abound; try to offer a rich nuance during the filigree work (at bars 58–61, for example), and take care with the many French musical terms, *passionnément*, *ironique*, *gracieux* and *marqué*, for example.

Tempo changes are specifically marked. Practice with a metronome until assured, then you can relax the pulse adding fluctuations for the desired effect.

The *staccato* notes are usually beneath slurs, so are not true *staccato*s, though they still need to be different from smooth notes. Imbue an intense character, for an authentic Spanish feel.

Tip

Piano and *pianissimo* make regular appearances. These markings both necessitate a deep touch, with fingers descending to the keybed for a focused sound. Less arm-weight and an intuitive sense of finger activity or control will prove helpful when distinguishing between them. Observe your finger movement during delicate passages, noting how much weight is required to sound notes, and, most importantly, listen for the differences needed to produce a brighter *piano* or a more muted *pianissimo*.

La puerta del Vino

No. 3 from **Préludes (Book 2), L. 123**

Claude Debussy (1862–1918)

Rubato
pp
più p
p marqué
pp sempre
sim.
mf
dim.
p

passionnément
au Mouvt
f âpre
f
ff
ff
Ped.
ironique
mf
dim.
p
p
Gracieux
p
p
sim.
pp
En retenant
p
più p
au Mouvt
pp
Ped.
simile

69
74
molto dim.
pp
79
mp
pp
pp
Un peu retardé
pp lointain
84
au Mouvt
ff
molto
p
pp
Ped.
p
pp

Prelude in B minor

Alexander Scriabin (1871–1915)

Scriabin's Preludes Op. 11 *follow Chopin's cycle (Op. 28) in their organisation (cycling through all 24 keys), and there are also some stylistic similarities too. The* Preludes Op. 11 *consist of a series of short pieces depicting different moods; No. 6 is a darkly dramatic, intensely turbulent work, which provides the perfect opportunity for pianists to display their octave technique.*

Set up

Key: B minor
Time signature: 2/4
Tempo: *Allegro:* ♩ = 168
Style: Late Romantic/ early Twentieth Century
Technical Focus: Octaves, chords, quick movement, and a powerful sound.

PREPARATION

As always, the scale and arpeggio in the key of the piece is a good place to begin. B minor has yet to be studied in this series. The harmonic minor is printed here, but it may be prudent to learn the melodic scale too. Practice slowly, with a full sound over four octaves. Aim to focus on the left hand, allowing it to speak above the right; this is a great way to implement finger strength.

Now play the left hand *fortissimo* and the right *pianissimo*, then reverse. There are many possible combinations; start the scale with both hands at a *mezzo-forte* dynamic, with the left hand gradually increasing in volume to a *fortissimo* at the top of the scale before returning to *mezzo-forte*, and the right decreasing to *pianissimo* at the top of the scale, *crescendo*-ing back to *mezzo-forte* at the end. This encourages refined practice and focused concentration.

A prerequisite for this piece is the ease with which octaves must be played. Opening the hand comfortably to play an octave can take some practice. Keeping the octave shape without any tension can be taxing for the smaller hand, and a larger hand sometimes requires greater flexibility as well.

Once you have practiced the exercises in the technique section for hand flexibility, let's work at the following. Play an octave in both hands, and ensure your wrists and arms are very relaxed as you hold the octave shape. It can be helpful to drop the wrist, lower than the level of the keyboard to aid relaxation throughout the body. As a rule, the piano

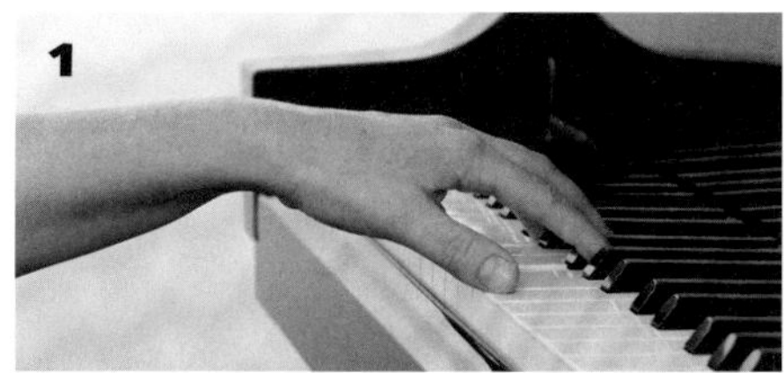

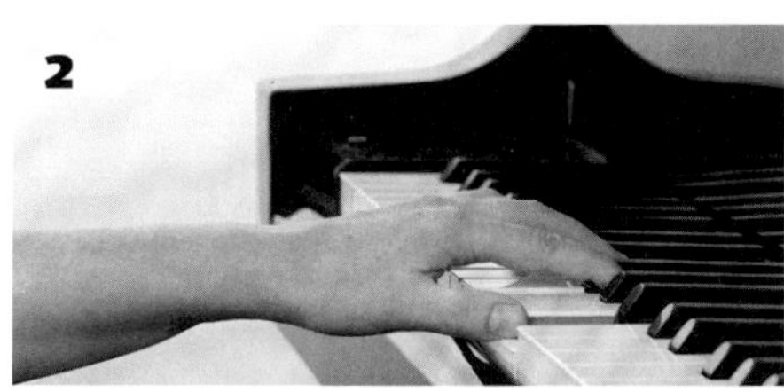

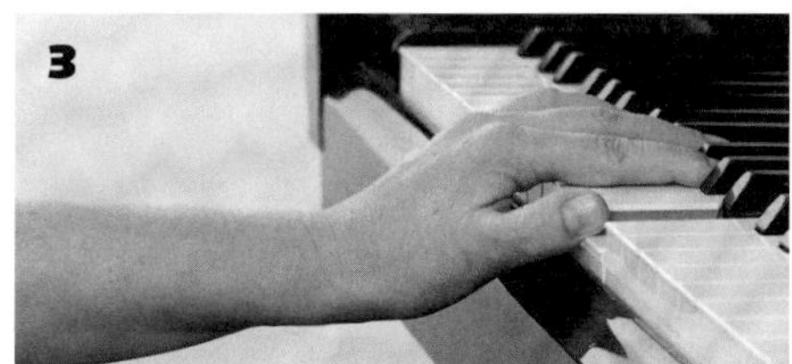

should never be played with a high or low wrist, as it must always be relaxed and ready to move, supporting the hand and fingers. But for practice purposes, this technique can help the hand and wrist relax whilst holding the shape: the photos here demonstrate three stages of playing an octave with a loose, some might say 'collapsed', wrist for purposes of relaxation. After the third photograph (at the bottom), let go of any tension in your hand and wrist, while still depressing the keys.

Once you feel flexible and loose, try to hone finger strength by playing the thumb and fifth finger on its 'tip'. It's never ideal to 'grip' a chord or octave as this implies rigidity, but if you can encourage the outer fingers and the thumb to form, and keep, a reliable shape (that of the Bridge position, with the knuckles visible), so that the hand learns the position, then this will help with accuracy. I advise students to play on the tip of the fifth finger particularly, as this is prone to collapsing.

Practicing octave shapes

Octaves move around at great speed throughout and it can be challenging to jump consistently and accurately for two pages. Practice two or four bars at a time, focusing on your movements. Forearms and elbows should ideally remain relaxed, and provide support to the wrist and hand. Let's look at this passage (bars 1–4):

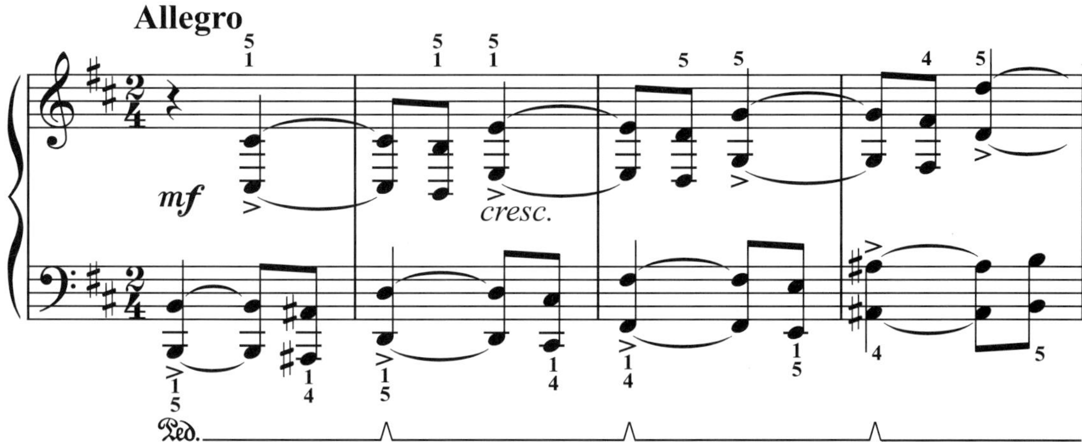

Practicing each part alone can be helpful; first, the top line of an octave, then the bottom line, especially if you watch finger positions and assimilate the movements slowly. Repeated note patterns can be surprisingly beneficial too, for example, playing each part of the octave alone in repeated sixteenth (semiquaver) notes; also, try repeating in duplets, triplet and quadruplets.

Off beats (marked with boxes) can be lighter, acting as an upbeat to the accented main beats:

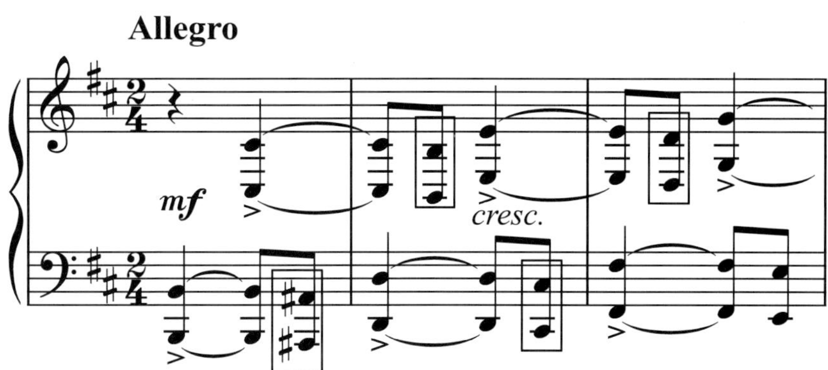

Practice moving swiftly from one octave to the next, and try working at double the expected speed in very short bursts:

Become accustomed to 'leading' your movements with the thumb; this can offer a sense of grounding, as it can be more secure than the outer fingers. However, when you feel confident, move on to leading with the outer fingers. To stop any 'over shooting' (landing further than you need) observe the outer fingers as you play: they will eventually be able to gauge the distances between the leaps, such as at bar 4, the second eighth note (quaver) to beat 2, as shown in the example.

PRACTICE TECHNIQUES

Right-hand practice

Ensure thorough practice when learning the note patterns, many leaps, and awkward movements. Memorisation will definitely help, so aim to be able to play through each hand separately without the score.

From bar 5, the right-hand inner melody appears and must come to the fore; practice the octave patterns alone before adding this inner voice. This musical line can add stability to the hand, because it is played on the first beat of the bar. Remain supple during the finger twisting which is sometimes involved in order to play quickly and fluently, such as at bars 40–44. The inner voice is marked with a circle in the example:

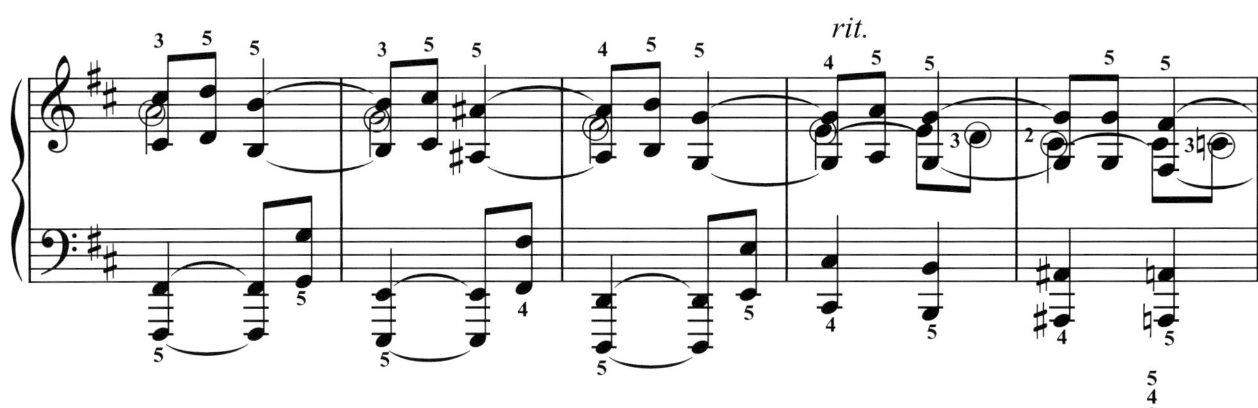

By practicing slowly, and gently feeding the inner voice into the octave shape, you will be able to adjust to this extra finger demand. The illusion of *legato* might be useful for the inner voice at bars 40–44, but the pedal will also help in this respect too. Chord passages are dramatic, often requiring leaps, such as at bars 17–18, as shown in the adjacent example.

Take the passage out of context. Play the chord at bar 18, beat 2, alone, with a full tone, ensuring all notes are sounding, especially the top E♭, which is important in the texture. Try the bottom and top lines alone (as marked in Nos. 1 and 2 in the example below). Then work at the preceding octave (a G), moving swiftly in an upward flowing movement, in order to 'catch' the G and the following chord in one swoop, almost akin to a drop-roll motion (No. 3), descending where the arrow is marked downwards, rolling up with the upward arrow, almost 'catching' the chord with your fingers as you roll upwards:

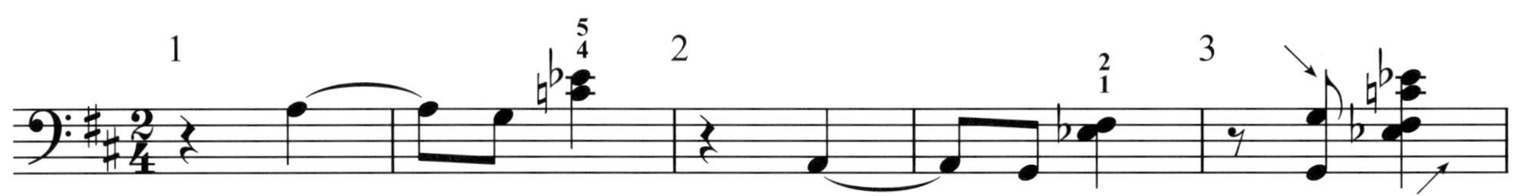

This can be a useful technique for all larger chords preceded by octaves. The octave should ideally be lighter than the chord. Octave movement in the bass clef played by the right hand might feel uncomfortable, at bars 17 and 18 for example; to counteract this, shift or lean slightly to the left, so you are not blocking hand and arm movements with your body.

Left-hand practice

Identical practice techniques apply to the left hand as that for the right, but the lower line must offer an even firmer beat and tonal support. Accents are crucial to the shape and flow of the piece, and chromatic bass lines (bars 43–46) can be highlighted.

The leaps and chord position changes from bars 31–34 and 38–43 will need isolated work; memorise the position changes, so that you can play each octave or chord without looking at the keyboard or your hands. Aim to 'sense' position changes.

> **Tip**
>
> Keep the wrists supple and relaxed throughout. Sooner or later they will enjoy feeling loose as the fingers take control, and working with the hand, learn the shape and angle necessitating economical movement.

Hands together

Finding places to break tension during the many octave and chordal passages is a recurrent issue throughout this book. There are many methods of doing this, but we will explore the following.

Breaking tension during octave and chord passages

After each octave movement, loosen and relax the wrists, keeping in mind the fact that once a note has been played on the piano, nothing more can be done to change the sound, so you can release all your tension, whilst still holding on to the notes or chords (as in bars 1 and 2):

After you've played the first C♯ octave (right hand), relax the wrist by lowering it, but keep the notes depressed. Repeat this practice suggestion with the left hand from bar 1, beat 1. Once the left hand has played the A♯ (bar 1, beat 2, second eighth note), move to the D, and relax the wrist again; when practicing, you may want to take the hands off the keyboard and rest them at this point. Now do this with the right-hand passage; after the octave E (bar 2, beat 2), rest the hand so it doesn't tire. You could mark up designated places for a wrist and hand rest, releasing tension (bars 35–39):

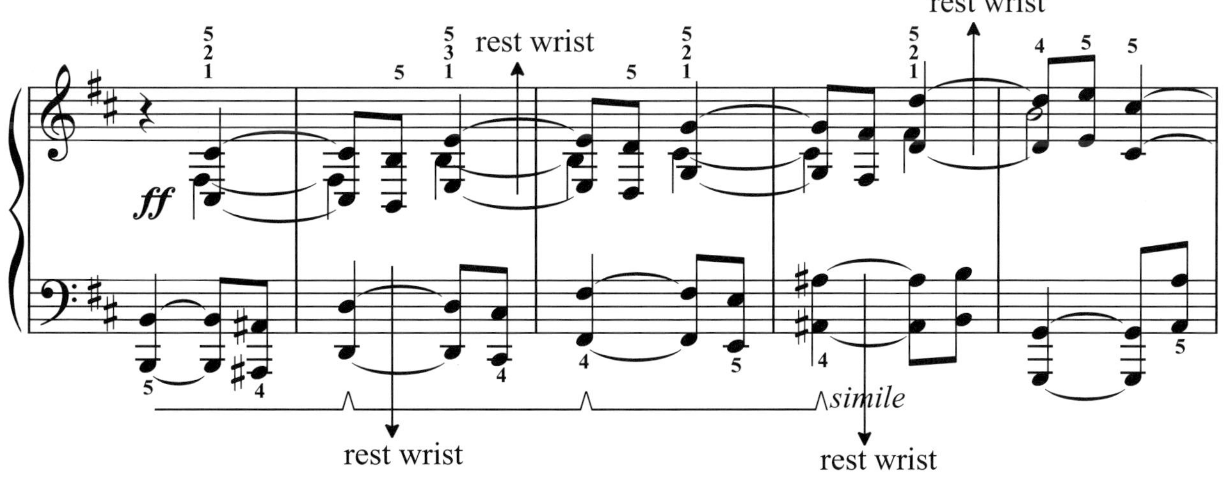

Now mark these constant breaks into the whole piece. This technique works well when practicing slowly, but can still be implemented when moving at speed. The rests or pauses become shorter and there will be less of them too, so the passages can be played in time. However, the wrist doesn't forget the feeling of the pauses or tension release moment, therefore the 'tension breaks' remain, but they can't be detected by anyone but the player. Eventually such passages can be elongated, so when playing at speed you may just need a rest at bar 8 (after the first chord, you can take a millisecond to breath at the end of the phrase) and bar 16 (first beat). Such tension release moments for the wrist can be applied at the end of each phrase.

Once securely hands together, bring out colour and a richer sound in the top and bottom lines of the texture, employing the fingerings you intend to use when playing all musical lines together (bars 8–10):

This involves playing with a deeper touch on the outer fingers, but this should be easier after practicing octave shapes. Coordination is vital, and it can be demanding to place each octave on the beat. Speed and confidence comes from knowing exactly where you are moving next, which is why slow practice is so beneficial.

The last chord can be either played as suggested – the top note taken by the left hand (moving over the right), and the lower octave being placed just before the beat. Or it could be played as in the example below; again, the lower octave played before the beat (marked with a bracket) but the upper notes being redistributed:

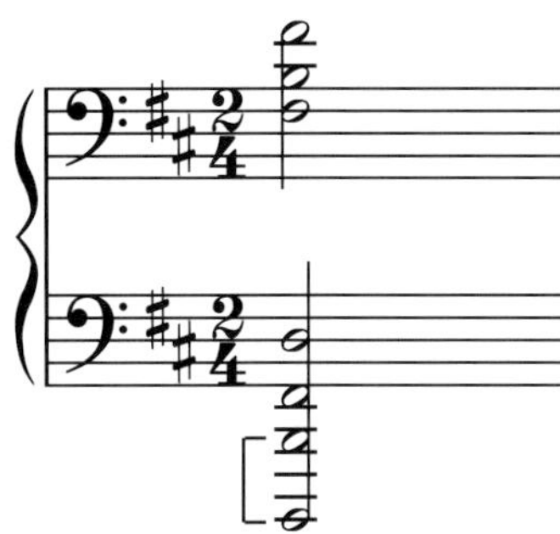

Tip

Both hands will benefit from slow metronome practice. You could use an eighth-note beat, placing each octave with the 'tick' (try eighth note equals 132 beats per minute) or even a sixteenth-note beat for more precision. Either way, raise the tempo very gradually, and play on the beat at all times.

INTERPRETATION

This prelude is in Ternary form; A (bars 1–16), B (bars 17–34), and A (bars 35–58). It's written in an etude-like style and the melodic material is formed from alternating longer notes which have been split between the hands. The resulting suspensions cause many harmonic dissonances providing a deeply impassioned character. With this in mind, it's prudent to keep a firm grip on tempo (too fast, and the musical line will be lost), and also, be aware of the many accents; some will be more important than others, but they will contribute to the intensity required for a satisfying interpretation.

Whilst practicing this work at a *forte* (loud) dynamic is a good method for building stamina, it is not necessary to assume full power throughout. There are places to employ softer dynamics (at bar 17 and 21, for example). With this in mind, work at a variety of tonal colours.

The pedal can be used liberally (as marked), and is the ideal way to reinforce accented chords. The *ritenuto* at bars 43–50 is important, as is the pause at bar 50, before an intensely dynamic, compelling final eight bars.

Tip

Scriabin was influenced by Synesthesia, associating various colours with harmonic tones and keys. According to his colour chart, B minor signified blue, which may indicate a mournful intensity certainly found in this work.

Prelude in B minor

Op. 11 No. 6

Alexander Scriabin (1871–1915)

rit.
rit.
rit.
simile
m.s.

Interludium and Fuga decima in D♭

Paul Hindemith (1895–1963)

Ludus Tonalis *(Tone Games) is a monumental work. Written in 1942, it contains a set of 12 fugues which are interconnected by 11 interludes, framed by a prelude and postlude. The work comprises all 12 major and minor keys and was intended to be a Twentieth-Century equivalent of J.S. Bach's* Well-Tempered Clavier. *Full of symmetry, the key system is a cycle of diminishing intervals surrounding C.*

Interludium

PREPARATION

For the scale and arpeggio of D♭ major, return to Book 2, page 95. This work may be devoid of a key-signature, but as can happen in Twentieth-Century music, the five flats have usually been added into the score.

A useful way to prepare might be to start by understanding the complex rhythmic patterns. They may look tricky at first, but there are copious patterns and sequences. Try to separate the rhythmic pulse from the music, working it out mentally and physically, before touching the keyboard. The pulse, of 60 eighth notes (quavers) per minute, is extremely slow, and this speed must be adhered to in order to capture the beautiful, yet intangible character.

Tap the following rhythm, featuring bars 1 and 2, on the piano lid, sub-dividing the beat to count sixteenth notes (semiquavers) as shown below, keeping a firm pulse to allow the shortest note values to be articulated easily. Use a metronome if it helps. Once secure, resume the eighth note beat.

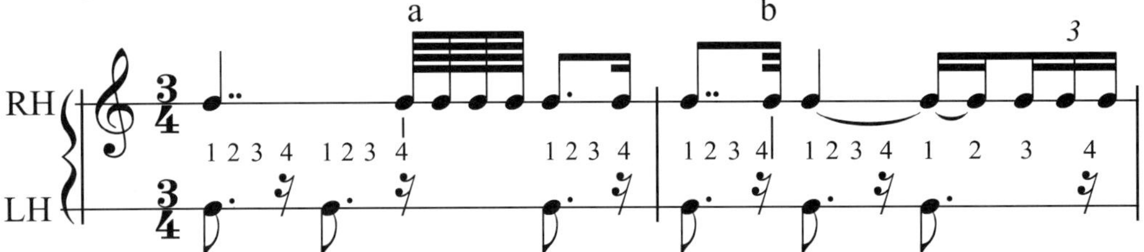

Move on the fourth sixteenth note beat of the second quarter (crotchet) note, which is marked with an 'a'. In bar 2, move after the fourth sixteenth note beat of the first quarter note; marked with a 'b'.

All dotted eighth notes at bars 5 and 6 will be played on the second sixteenth beat of each count of four, within the quarter note beat. When you tap the rhythms, ensure you let each note fully sound, without rushing the end of a beat.

The addition of the left hand should ideally stabilise the pulse. If you use a metronome, listen in between the 'tick' so you can judge the amount of time available before the next beat in order to place sixty-fourth notes (hemidemisemiquavers) as at bar 1.

Set up

Key: D♭ major
Time signature: 3/4
Tempo: *Molto tranquillo*: ♪ = 60
Style: Twentieth Century
Technical Focus: Precise rhythm, articulation and chromatic colour.

PRACTICE TECHNIQUES

Right-hand practice

Once the rhythm has been grasped, go through the piece locating the appropriate note patterns. I have added some fingering to the score which will hopefully be useful, but you may also like to consider the following for bar 1:

And the following for bars 8–10:

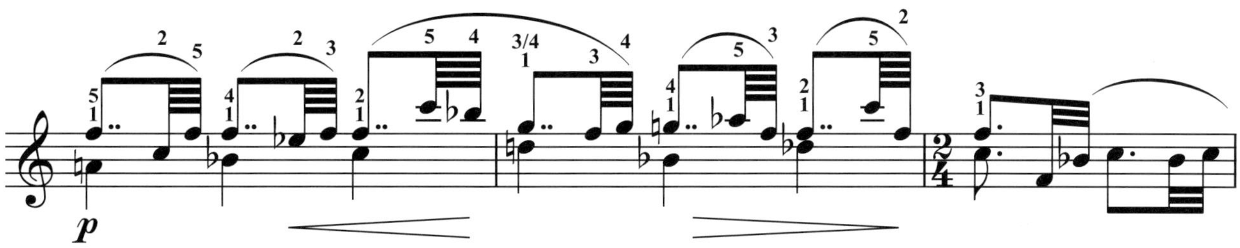

Hand position changes require quick movement, despite the slow tempo. In this instance, it can be beneficial to work at the movements in isolation, for example between beats 1 and 2 at bar 6 (C♭ to F♭), and at beat 2, bar 18 (F to E♭). Change swiftly from one to the next with a quick wrist and forearm motion, landing firmly, with a decisive tone, until the position change is assured.

Repetition is the surest method for learning passages with constantly changing accidental patterns. You may need to repeat each bar 10–20 times before the fingers digest the patterns.

Note the 3/8 time signature in bar 15.

Tip

The act of changing fingers whilst keeping a note depressed will be a repeated technique throughout. Irrespective of how you change fingers, aim to ensure that the notes remain firmly in place, holding the *legato* line, which is necessary almost for the entire piece.

Left-hand practice

The left-hand chords can be punctuated by lifting-off at the end of each one precisely, observing sixteenth note rests. This forms part of the detached character, contrasting with the *legato* touch in the right hand.

Balancing chords

The left-hand chords must be well-coordinated so that each note sounds together. Once fingering and note patterns are secure, play the second chord in bar 1 (an A♭ and B♭) and depress both keys at the same time, without sounding the note, that is, rest your fingers on the keys, taking them down into the key bed very slowly, feeling the double escapement action or point where a note can repeat (on a grand piano) without fully releasing the key.

Experiment by playing the two notes, one after another, observing how slowly you need to play for a very soft tone. This takes some practice, and the results will change depending on the instrument. The difference between the notes sounding or not is a fraction of a movement, so careful judgement is crucial.

When you eventually play the two notes together, balance your finger positions, so that the notes are given equal weight. When practicing four-note chords, especially when the fourth finger is involved, ensure extra arm weight is employed, in order to achieve equal balance between the fingers and thumb (if the thumb is used).

Hands Together

Employing a firmer touch on the short notes will provide shape and rhythmic colour. Experiment with the following different articulation suggestions. In the second example (bar 5), pay attention to the last triplet note (marked with an arrow), so that it fully sounds, and isn't rushed.

The accents or *tenuto* markings are for practice purposes; 'placing' the beats with a structural and rhythmic awareness should be sufficient.

The contemplative thematic melody returns in part at bar 11, and will benefit from a deeper, more sonorous tone on its second appearance.

INTERPRETATION

Minimal pedalling has been added, but some will be necessary in order to tastefully colour the melody and add sonority to the left-hand chords. Mark your own pedalling in the score, bearing in mind the many short note values which might need partial pedalling (see page 148) or flutter pedalling. Add touches of pedal at bars 19 and 20, but be sure to release the pedal in time for the last two sixty-fourth notes of each quarter note beat.

Set up

Key: D♭ major
Time signature: 4/4
Tempo: *Allegro moderato, grazioso*: ♩ = 72
Style: Twentieth Century
Technical Focus:
Contrapuntal playing, rhythmic precision, and *legato.*

Fuga Decima

PREPARATION

As with the *Interludium*, the challenges in this fugue are often rhythmic. The pulse might remain four quarter notes per bar, but within that framework numerous note patterns must be precisely counted and executed. As before, work through bar by bar marking a suitable pulse into the score, which enables easy sub-division. It's always useful to set exceedingly slow practice speeds, in order to place short notes.

STRUCTURE

Spend time examining the structure before learning the notes (for more information on fugues, see Book 2, pg. 89 and 94). The three-part fugue contains three musical lines; the subject or theme appears in bar 1 (in the middle voice, marked as Subject Entry 1 below), bar 3 (top line in the dominant; Entry 2) and bar 6, (bottom line; Entry 3).

The countersubject also appears in bar 3, as marked above. Look out for the two *stretti* between the top and middle voice at bars 12 and 15. The first section finishes at bar 18, with all three voices in unison on an A♭:

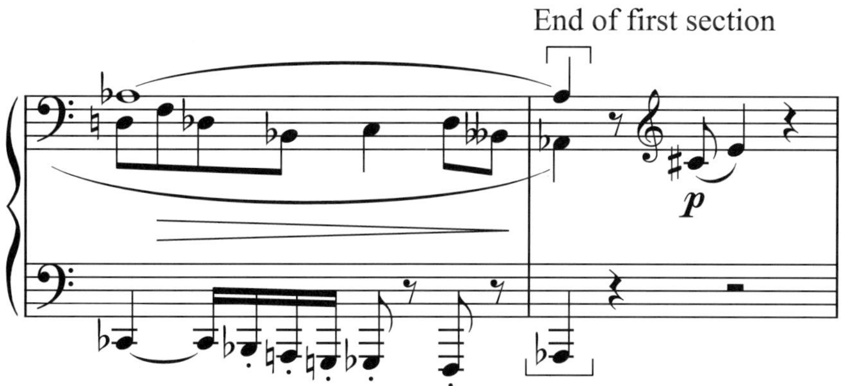

The whole fugue inverts from bar 18, often written enharmonically, and ends with the subject stated in its original form at bar 34 in the left hand (lower voice).

PRACTICE TECHNIQUES

Right-hand practice

As with most fugues, separate hand practice is key and will be of utmost importance when solidifying fingering and note patterns. Start by separating the musical lines, paying attention to the articulation which must be consistent throughout each fugal entry.

Think of all three voices as separate entities. You might consider writing the piece out in open score, which will really aid learning (bars 34–36):

Practicing Counterpoint

1 Divide the fugue into small sections.

2 As mentioned, work at the voices one at a time, but **only** use the fingering you intend when playing all the parts together.

3 Slow tempos are the best method of assimilation, but when more confident increase the speed gradually.

4 Practice two voices at a time in all combinations.

5 Now change the sound; *forte* in one voice, *mezzo-forte* in the second, and *piano*, for the third (there are many possible combinations).

6 For a real challenge try different articulation combinations too, for example, *staccato* in voice one, *non-legato* for voice two, and *legato*, for voice three. Voicing needs care when jumping between the hands.

7 The act of holding a voice down whilst letting go and moving with another, all in the same hand, can cause issues. Some may find it useful to play one part and silently play the others; your fingers will feel the notes, but they won't depress the keys.

8 You will eventually need to decide which voice must be brought to the fore; it's all about layering and balancing the sound.

Left-hand practice

The left hand mostly plays one musical line throughout, with the exception of bars 6–9 and 12–14. Clarity is especially important from bar 15–18; pay attention to articulation, keeping a clear sound free from muddiness. Articulation may want for special practice in the bass, demanding crisp nuancing, in order to really hear the musical line alongside (and sometimes above) the upper voices.

Hands Together

Observe the rests. Breathing space is vital in a complex structure such as this, providing time between subject and countersubject entries, such as at bar 3, allowing the music to breath. Give the necessary time to 'place' notes and build intensity when appropriate.

INTERPRETATION

Dynamic colour can differentiate the voices, but there are few dramatic climaxes, with the exception of bar 12, and bar 28 and 29, which demand a fuller sound. Aim to use softer dynamics combined with specific articulation to develop your interpretation.

Tip

Pedalling has been marked at bars 12–13, 29–30, 33–36. This is primarily to retain notes which would otherwise be lost due to larger intervals. You may feel more pedalling is required to sustain certain chromatic harmony, but this should be executed with caution; Hindemith's austere style necessitates a dry approach, therefore let your fingers do the talking.

Interludium and Fuga decima in D♭

Paul Hindemith (1895–1963)

Fuga decima in D♭

Allegro moderato, grazioso ♩ = 72

cresc.
mf
mp
f
Ped.
p
p

23
p
cresc.
26
mf
mp
28
f
Ped.
30
p
33
dim.
pp
Ped.
Ped.

Frenzy: Étude for Nimble Fingers

Melanie Spanswick (b. 1969)

Composed in December 2017, Frenzy is an Étude written for the purpose of improving articulation. An Étude or study is a technical challenge, often focusing on one specific issue; the smoothness required to play the continuous sixteenth note (semiquaver) passages will determine the success of a performance.

Set up

Key: A minor
Time signature: $\frac{4}{4}$
Tempo: *Maestoso:* ♩ = 80
Presto: ♩ = 152–160
Style: Minimalist/ Contemporary
Technical Focus: Clarity, articulation, coordination, rhythm, and lateral wrist movement.

PREPARATION

To reacquaint with the key of A minor, return to Book 1 (page 19) for the scale and arpeggio. The texture of this piece is fairly simple. Start by playing the notes in each bar altogether as groups, or as one chord. You may have to change position, such as in bars 5–8:

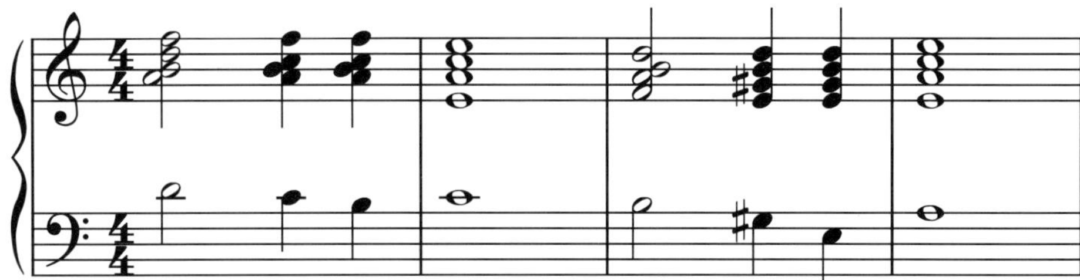

You can work through the entire piece this way. Each position change (for example, at bars 44–45) will require precision and the difficulty is to reposition the hand swiftly, so it's ready for the next note pattern without disturbing the last sixteenth note (semiquaver) of the previous four-note pattern. Once you can play through the entire piece slowly, be aware of the various pattern changes, or where sixteenth notes change direction for a few bars; as at bars 15–17, for example.

Tip

Mark the various chord progressions into the score, noting the chromatic chords or less familiar chord patterns. Identifying chord structure and harmonic changes will benefit interpretation and memorisation.

PRACTICE TECHNIQUES

Right-hand practice

The opening chords are *Maestoso*. With this in mind, try to colour the inner parts as it's in the middle of each chord where the intensity and melodic interest lies. Practice the inner intervals alone (example 1), and put more emphasis on each inner note separately (examples 2 and 3), and then on both inner notes. With the finger tips, touch and press deeply into the keys, keeping the outer octaves (the As), slightly lighter. Eventually, you will be able to adjust and balance the colour of each chord accordingly, but always keep in mind the inner melodies.

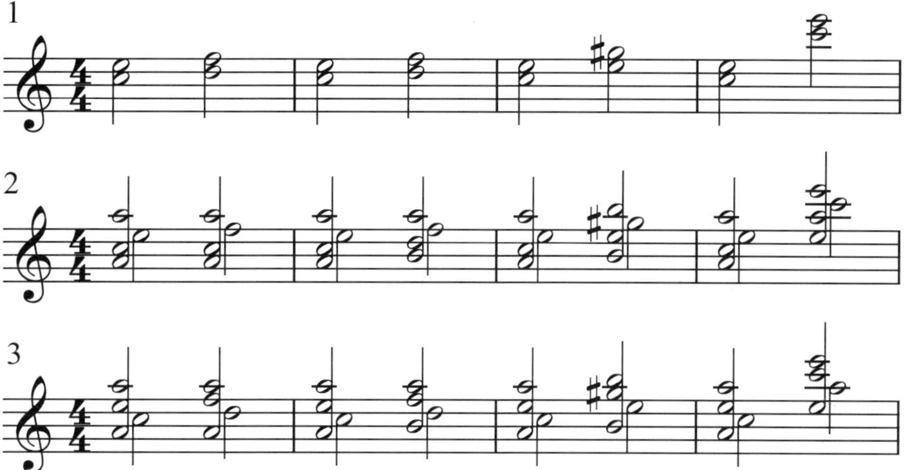

Lateral Wrist Movement

Lateral wrist motion will prove very beneficial when playing this piece, in order to play every sixteenth note evenly and rhythmically, and also to move in a fluid manner from one note group to the next. Note or chord patterns generally last for a bar, before the need to change hand positions; aim to keep the wrist loose and malleable, although the fingers must remain firm. Wrist – arm alignment is an important topic, however, when note patterns are widespread and speed is involved, one comfortable method of moving across the keys is to use lateral wrist movement.

In photo 1, my fifth finger plays the first note in bar 6 (E), with my wrist positioned to the right, away from the body. I then move the wrist and arm slowly towards my body; it gradually progresses through a 'central' position moving to the left, as it plays the C and A. In the second photo, I have moved the wrist and arm fully to the left, with my thumb placed on the E. Try to let the arm guide the hand and wrist. Keep the wrists flexible, avoiding any stiffness. You may find it necessary to add a slight circular or rotational wrist movement here too, which will facilitate speed (for more about circular wrist motion, revisit the Technique section of Book 1 and 2).

Work at each sixteenth-note group slowly, focusing on the inner notes. Tonal and rhythmic evenness will be important. The following example features the opening bar of the *Presto* (bar 5). Use your fingertips, with a deep touch; much deeper than that with which you will eventually play the piece. Here are some practice ideas:

The thumb should ideally softly brush the keys at the bottom of each downward figuration, but it must be sure to 'place' the final fourth sixteenth note carefully. However, when the pattern is reversed (as in bars 21–22), it must assume control, sounding the strong beat. The overall balance between the fingers is vital.

Here are some suggestions for working on the second and third finger:

These can be applied throughout the piece. It's easy to rush or 'swallow' the last sixteenth note in every pattern, therefore count in sixteenth notes. The fifth finger must quickly assume the position for the next group, but by focusing on the rhythm and allowing every note to speak, you will be aware of the final note in each pattern and will resist any urge to rush. Practicing in various rhythms can be helpful too.

The first note of every group will require a 'placing' and perhaps a slight leaning (or *tenuto*) touch. Patterns such as that at bars 18–20 will benefit from a more circular rotational wrist movement. Move the wrist towards the body for the first two sixteenth notes of each group (C followed by an A), marked by the arrow, in the example below, then move outwards, away from the body, whilst the fingers are playing the final C and A of each group.

Lateral Motion

The pattern at bar 24 should feel more comfortable after developing a firmer finger touch in the fourth and fifth finger, as suggested:

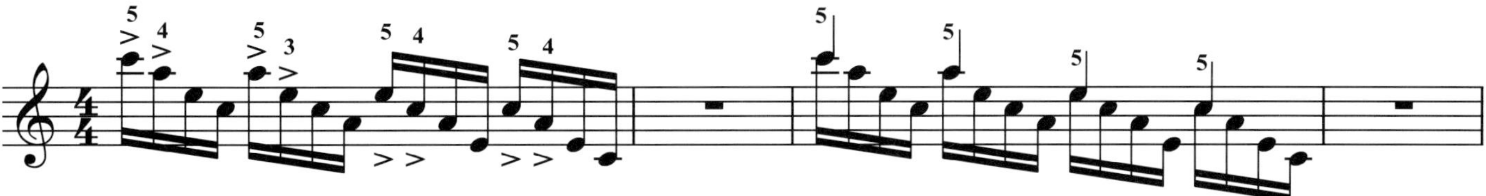

Aim for key depth when strengthening these fingers, but avoid any strain or tension. Keep the hand and arm from uncomfortable locking up by relaxing, or freeing, the wrist at suitable points in the music, regularly releasing the muscles.

From bar 39, the right hand assumes the melody in octaves. Whilst pedal has been suggested, some of the octave passagework is marked without pedal, and therefore will need to be joined for a smooth musical line. Work at the outer octave notes in four-bar phrases, until you can join the notes seamlessly using a *legato* illusion. Keep the fifth finger depressed until the very last moment, lifting it at lightning speed to play the subsequent note, matching the sound carefully. Repeat this process until you can barely hear any gaps. During bars 39–57, allow your thumb to 'ground' each octave for control, and try to phrase the melody with plenty of dynamic gradation.

Left-hand practice

From bars 5–24 the left hand has the starring role. The melody should ideally consist of a full *cantabile*. Let's examine the first four-bar phrase. Whilst *pianissimo* is marked in bar 5, in order to project a soft timbre, you will need to engage the thumb fully, and play into the key, touching and pressing to produce the necessary sound required of a melody line. It can help to play the melody with many different dynamics, experimenting with sound and colour. This is one possible dynamic interpretation:

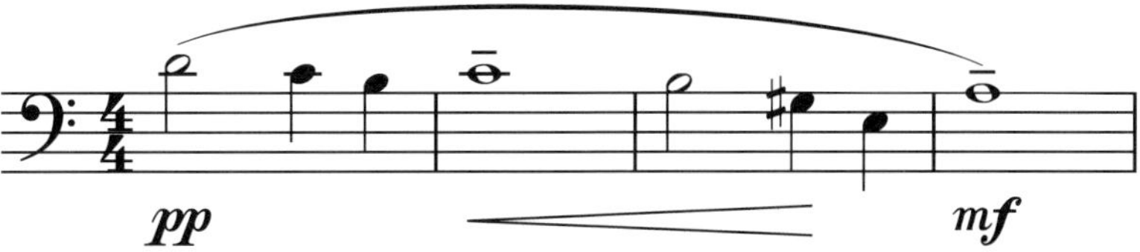

In bar 7, the thumb must turn lightly and match the sound of the preceding middle C (bar 6), and the final A is certainly the most powerful note in the phrase.

In a similar manner to the right hand, the left-hand accompaniment will be more effective with a strong fourth finger, so the following exercise may help (bar 40):

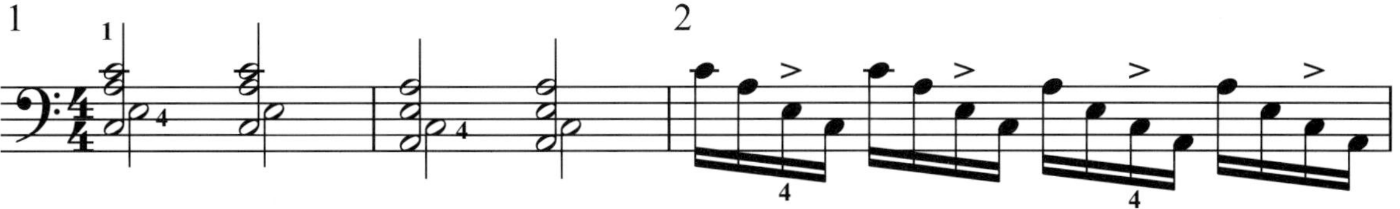

Weight the fourth finger so it can be clearly heard above the other notes. Lift the finger, to lightly tap the note, whilst keeping the other notes depressed (1). Finally, accent the finger with several touches (2) including accents, *non-legato* and *staccato*. This should never feel tense or uncomfortable. Aim to use this practice tool throughout the piece.

Hands together
It's advisable to use three metronome speeds for various stages of practice: a slow speed, perhaps a sixteenth note equals 200 beats per minute, a mid-speed, quarter note (crotchet) equals 76 beats per minute, and a much faster tempo, quarter note equals 152 beats per minute.

Bars 26–61 sometimes combine sixteenth notes in both hands; the success of these passages all depends on learning the fingering fastidiously, followed by detailed rhythmic practice for perfect coordination. Here are some ideas based on bar 48:

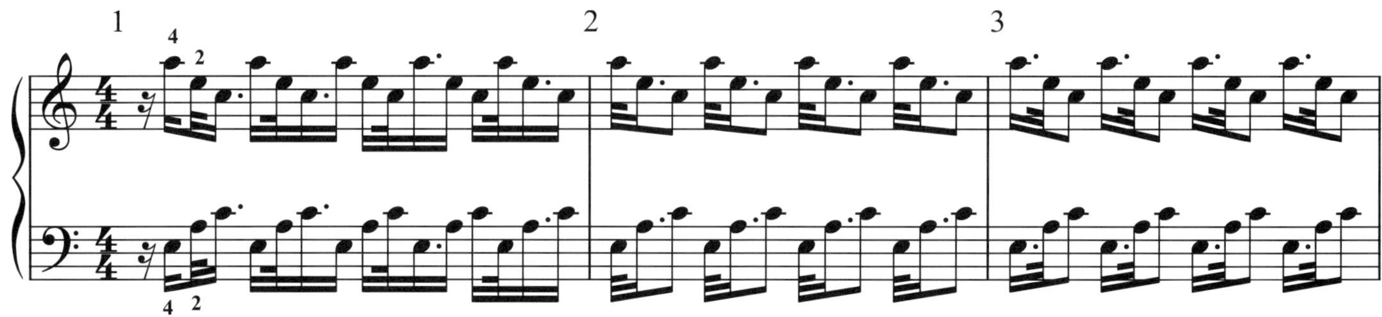

When even and fluent, aim to practice the example above including the two whole note (semibreve) Cs, which are to be held throughout the bar. These ideas might also be useful from bars 58–61, where *tremolo*-like (a shake) patterns could be practiced with plenty of emphasis on the weaker fingers. Once rapid passagework has been worked at with a heavy finger touch, lighten your touch, for even, rhythmical sixteenth notes. Practice the piece without the sustaining pedal.

INTERPRETATION

A bell-like quality pervades the opening chords (and those in bars 54–57). To achieve this, think about a rich sonority on the bass notes, between every chord; each one should ideally be played more powerfully than the last. Less is more regarding the sustaining pedal. If you can join melody lines with finger *legato*, so much the better. However, if you feel more pedal is necessary, ensure quick changes and a 'flutter' approach.

Keep the 'frenzied' character by employing a fairly swift pulse and as little *rubato* as possible.

Tip

Be sure to depress the sustaining pedal in the last two bars, as it provides a hazy effect and a rather mysterious ending.

Frenzy: Étude for Nimble Fingers

Melanie Spanswick (b. 1969)

18
21
f
ff
24
p
Ped.
27
30
Ped.
33
f
Ped.
Ped.

rit.
a tempo
mf
p
f
Ped.

49
Ped.
51
rit.
54
ff
a tempo
fff
59
f
61
mp
8b

Sonata in C minor (Pathétique)

Ludwig van Beethoven (1770–1827)

Set up

Key: C minor
Time signature: C *(Grave)* and ¢ *(Allegro di molto e con brio)*
Tempo: *Grave:* ♪ = 56
Allegro di molto e con brio: 𝅗𝅥 = 126
Style: Classical
Technical Focus:
Rhythmic precision, *tremolo* figurations, quick movement around the keyboard, tonal contrast, and ornamental passagework.

Beethoven wrote this celebrated work in 1798, and it was published in 1799. It has remained one of his most popular sonatas. Originally called Grande sonate pathétique, *it's believed to be one of the few sonatas that Beethoven named himself. Consisting of three movements, each one displays typical Beethovenian qualities, not least the tragedy, drama, and expressivity which are present throughout.*

First movement Grave – Allegro di molto e con brio

Tip

This sonata is an example of the Classical style, demanding clean lines, precise finger work, and clear articulation. Listen attentively to every eighth note (quaver) passage, and articulate with clarity and eloquence.

PREPARATION

For the scale and arpeggio in the key of C minor, return to Book 1, page 58.

The first movement is set in Sonata Form. This is a musical structure consisting of three fundamental sections: an exposition, a development, and a recapitulation. Themes are presented in the exposition (bars 1–132), this is followed by a development section (bars 133–194), where they are often embellished or contrasted. The recapitulation (bars 195–310) resolves the thematic material, both harmonically and thematically, and a coda (bars 295–310) rounds the movement off. It may help to analyse the work away from the keyboard, marking themes and harmonic structure.

For a smooth, fluid line, aim to use as much *legato* in the *Grave* as possible. This can be done courtesy of the sustaining pedal, but it's much more effective to use the fingers. Let's work on *legato* fingering in bar 6 (beats 1–3). Such a passage could be played using the fifth finger throughout, on the upper note of each octave, but for a seamless join, try this fingering:

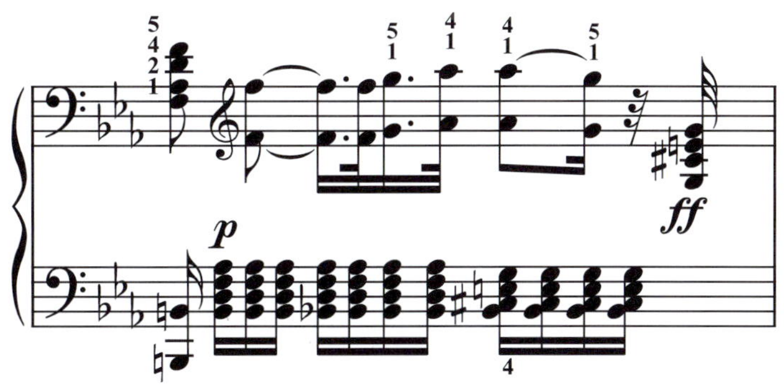

Play the outer parts alone, using the intended fingering:

The top line will need strong fingers and a deep touch. When putting both parts together, relax the hand and encourage a light, flexible thumb join. As always, weight the hand towards the weaker fingers. You might prefer a detached touch for some of the declamatory octave passages where slurs are not present, but a *legato* line helps keep momentum and promotes expressivity.

The Tremolo

A major technical challenge throughout (from bar 11) is the recurrent use of the *tremolo* figure. A *tremolo* literally means 'a trembling effect', where notes are played as rapidly as possible. Here, the *tremolo* patterns are written into the score with an eighth note rhythm, and require a very controlled specific movement. They last for many bars which can eventually lead to fatigue and tension.

Here are a few ideas to keep the rapid octave movements controlled and flexible at speed (bars 11–17):

Allegro di molto e con brio 𝅗𝅥 = 126

Start by marking the part, learning fingerings and octave shapes, bars 11–17:

Once secure, ensure your hand has formed a Bridge position between the thumb and fifth finger, as shown in the first photo below, where my knuckles can be seen. The fifth finger will need plenty of support, because it must be as strong and agile as the thumb. This type of octave passagework can be played efficiently when the fifth finger is encouraged to 'stand' on its tip (second photo) and the thumb is also fully engaged, ensuring note accuracy:

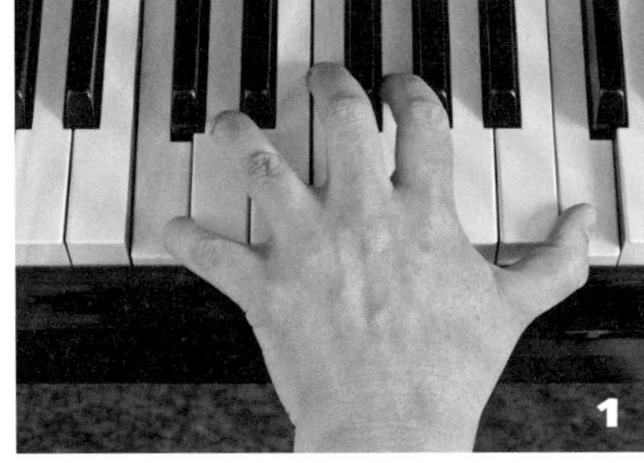
1

2

Slowly play each eighth note, accenting the lower note, as in example 1. Then reverse this with accents on the thumb. Accents will provide strength and a keen sense of rhythmic pulse at both slow and faster tempi. Finally, work at the second example in sixteenth notes (semiquavers) for firmer precision on the lower notes.

To play at speed, the hand will need to 'shake' or rotate from side to side. Practice by shaking your hand quickly in a small rotational movement from the wrist; from the fifth finger up to the thumb and back, as if turning a door knob!

Find places to break the tension, perhaps every half bar to begin with:

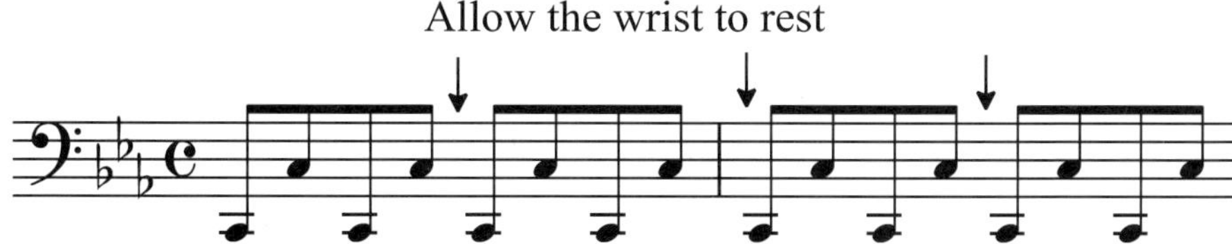

Play four eighth notes and take a break to release the hand and wrist, as marked. Eventually, aim to alleviate wrist tension by using a constantly moving wrist; a drop-rise motion, that is, dropping the wrist (and relaxing it briefly) on the last eighth note of a bar, rising up on the first beat of the following bar, can be beneficial.

The faster you play, so the breaks will eventually become much shorter, but the hand will be accustomed to the feeling of a rest and will implement it naturally. When up to speed, a useful place to release any stiffness in the wrists is bar 19 (after beat 1) and bar 27 (after beat 1), where the ends of phrases will benefit from an extra 'placing'.

The right-hand *tremolo* passages (bars 149–167) might require a heavier fifth finger (or fourth), therefore practice with more weight on the top of the hand, so when you come to play at speed, the hand will feel balanced. The top note of each *tremolo* figure must remain rhythmical, with no rushing or pushing of the beat, and this will depend on an even hand and wrist rotational movement for success.

PRACTICE TECHNIQUES

Right-hand practice

The *Grave* is a solemn, stately introduction. Top notes of each chord must be highlighted in order to carry the musical line. Work at the rapid passagework evenly and slowly, with a heavy touch, until fingerings and movements are secure and comfortable.

The final chromatic scale (bar 10), might benefit from shape and contour. Despite being one phrase, when practicing, add accents on a variety of different fingers, in order to strengthen them and eventually acquire rhythmic and tonal evenness. Chromatic scales generally benefit from a swift rotational hand movement (similar to turning a door knob) between each finger and thumb during practice, helping to develop rhythmic precision at speed.

From bar 11, the character, texture and speed changes. Chords, announcing the thematic material (or the first subject), can be worked at separately, always moving to the top of the phrase (bar 15 beat 1, for example). Work with a *legato* touch when practicing the patterns for clarity and focus, then add a light wrist *staccato* (see pages 121/2) when moving at speed. Bar 13, beat 2, must have a rich colour, as indicated by the *sforzando* marking.

To place these passages, aim to count in eighth note beats; for rhythmic precision, I find it helpful to count in sixteenth note beats when practicing slowly. Avoid rushing between position changes (bar 12, beats 1 and 2, bar 13, beats 2 and 4, and bar 14, beats 1 and 2).

Fast passages require shape when executed at speed. The following might be practiced like this (bars 29–30):

Accents and *tenuto* markings are useful tools, especially for slow practice, but when up to speed, less accentuation and a lighter touch will contour the passage, keeping it rhythmical and providing a sense of direction.

This type of spot practice will also benefit bars 113–120, 167–170 and 187–194.

A feature in this movement is the swift crossing of hands. In order to master this, work in chordal groups, moving quickly around the keyboard (the following example has been built on bars 51–57):

Try to play the left-hand part in chords too (see example above), and practice moving from one chord group to another, finding the position changes quickly.

Displacing octaves can be helpful as well:

When returning to the written score, implement *staccato* articulation by using the top of the finger in a 'scratching' motion, keeping very close to the keys, for accuracy.

Ornaments form an important part of the melodic material in the right hand. The mordents from bar 57 onwards are to be played like this (bar 57), 1 in the example. However, some might prefer 2, or even 3:

Sound each one on the beat, and aim to practice using a heavy touch keeping all notes even. Then lighten your touch on the second and third note, so that the ornament doesn't disrupt the rhythm. Ensure the quarter notes (crotchets) are paired together, employing a drop-roll movement for neat slurs (for more information about the drop-roll technique, please see Book 1 p. 30).

Left-hand practice
The left hand largely provides the accompaniment, yet requires ample power and support. In the *Grave*, it must use a deeper touch for chords from bars 5–8; all notes sounding together, therefore practice balancing the hand, depressing all the notes in one go, using substantial arm-weight, touching and pressing into the keys. As you touch the key surface, allow the wrist to act as a hinge, taking the weight of the arm behind the fingers. This should provide a rich sound devoid of any harshness.

Whole notes (semibreves) and half notes (minims) must be held firmly by the fifth, or occasionally fourth, finger from bars 51–92. Achieve the *legato* line by practicing without the upper parts, leaving the note depressed almost until the next one sounds.

In the development section, a left-hand motif might need careful articulation; bars 149–159. Quarter notes swiftly move up the keyboard using the drop-roll technique. The second note of each pair can be softer and not rushed, and ensure good ensemble with the right hand.

Hands together

Grave
The opening is both majestic and tragic. Repetitive chord structures need perfect rhythm. To make sure the short beats are in their rightful place, count in equal, even sixteenth notes, like this:

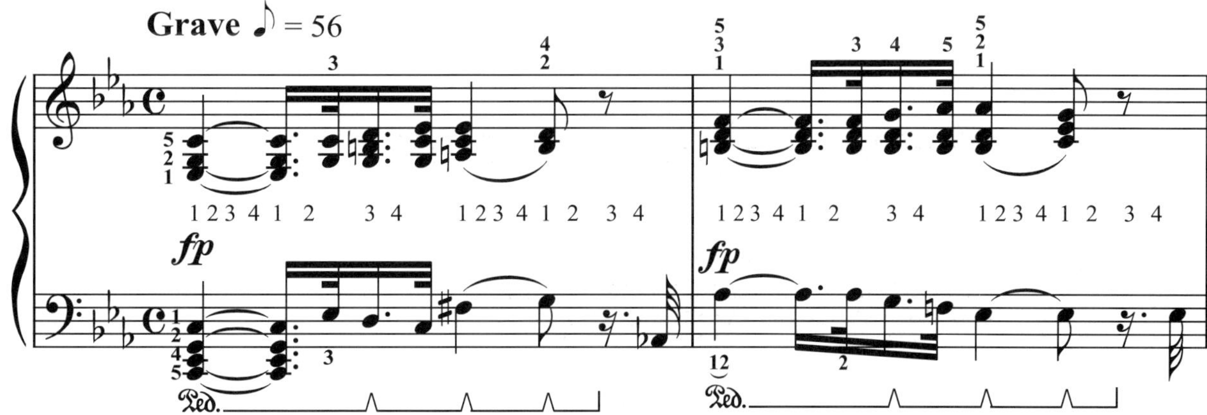

Place each beat deliberately, and most importantly, evenly, so there is no sense of rushing or lingering, the tempo should be strictly kept here. Take note of the sudden dynamic shifts, from *forte* to *piano* within the space of one beat.

Rests are vital. Observe each one; a short breath in bars 1 and 2 on beat 4, provides suspense and drama. Similarly, at bar 9 (beats 3 and 4), the rests may seem unnecessarily long, but if correctly counted, heighten the suspense and intensity.

Position changes from bars 5–8 will necessitate quick movement and good coordination. As with many position shifts around the keyboard, over-compensating, during practice, can have remarkable effects; aim to jump or move an octave further than actually written.

Allegro di molto e con brio
Coordination must be worked at carefully throughout. In order to account for every note rhythmically, set a slow metronome pulse; hopefully your left-hand *tremolos* now feel confident and fluent, and at slow speeds will be able to coordinate fully with the right-hand material. Slow work may need to be done for an extended period. Raise the speed gradually; when practicing, experiment with three different metronome speeds at each practice session (extremely slow, slow, and moderate pulses).

Fast Broken Passagework

Fast broken passagework dominates from bars 93–98 and bars 105–110. Such figurations with changing hand positions and emphasis on the outer fingers can cause tension. Let's break this down and work at it with relaxation and flexibility in mind. Here's the passage (from bar 93):

Learn in chords, moving slowly from one position change to the next:

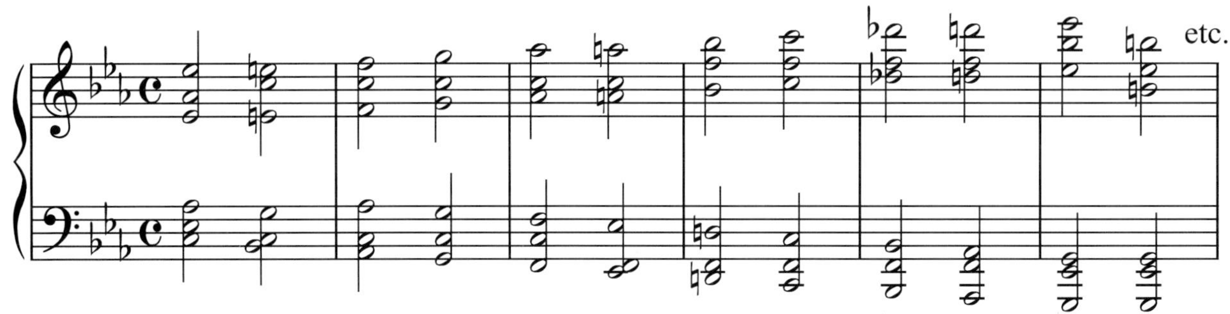

Now work at the inner parts. These must be crisply articulated; set a slow metronome pulse (perhaps eighth notes equal 104 beats per minute). As you play, note the hand position required and practice with a heavy touch. Turning to the outer parts, work at the melodic line and bottom of the harmony alone:

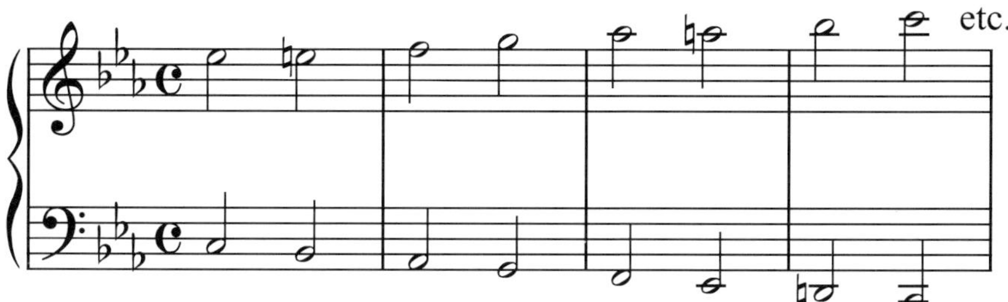

When playing together, use accents on the first and third beat of each group of four eighth notes:

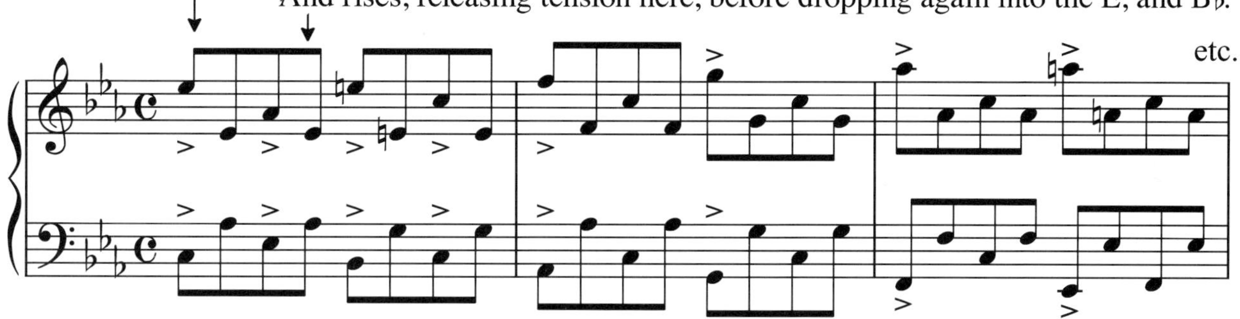

Employ a drop-rise technique for each half note group; this involves the wrist dropping into the first note of each group of four, and rising on the last eighth note of the group. If done slowly, this will allow a tension break for the wrist and hand.

As speed is added, keep the figurations light with the exception of the first note (marked *staccato*). Move at lightning speed from one hand position to another, and as you move consciously release any physical tension; this will require focus, but when implemented you will find this passage easier to play.

INTERPRETATION

Suggested pedalling has been marked throughout. The opening might well be played using the flutter pedalling (or half pedalling) technique. Experiment with this in bar 1; after the first chord, flutter the sustaining pedal, moving it rapidly up and down in small increments. As this is done, keep the chord still depressed with the fingers, clearing the sound until the appearance of the second chord (beat 2).

A combination of pedalling and finger pedalling may be effective for bar 4. Depress the sustaining pedal on beat 4, but for the very last group of nine notes, release it and use an overlapping finger pedal technique; where fingers keep notes depressed as subsequent notes are played, slightly overlapping the sound.

When pedalling *tremolos*, be aware of the constant movement, which may demand half pedalling or constant fluttering, depending on the instrument. The *staccato* passages (bar 9, beat 2 and bar 10, beat 2) can be articulated with a softer *non-legato* touch. Important melody notes, such as those at bar 4, beat 3 (the tied A♭), require a specific deeper tone and a rhythmical 'placing', providing a feeling of expectancy.

Shifting chord patterns and vague flirtations with different keys in the *Allegro di molto e con brio* might need definition on the top notes; for example from bars 207–218.

Sforzandos abound; never ignore them as they add vital punctuation to the profound musical sentences.

Tip

Beethoven is very specific about pauses and rests or fermatas. They are included for a reason; usually that of dramatic effect. As this is central to the meaning of this work, be sure to give every rest its full value, or even a little longer.

Second Movement
Adagio Cantabile

PREPARATION

For the scale and arpeggio in the key of A♭ major, see Book 2, page 59.

This serenely beautiful well-known movement provides a complete contrast, and offers the pianist a chance to really 'sing' at the keyboard. It also needs detailed attention to phrasing and a rich tonal palete. Set in Ternary form (A – B – A), the turbulent central section transforms briefly into the minor.

In the examples below, the three parts, or musical lines, have been written out separately. If you can think in layers and balance the sound, you will be well on the way to developing a secure interpretation:

The lower line (above), played by the left hand, must add depth, yet still be in the background tonally. Play each bar with a very smooth *legato* touch, transferring the weight from each finger evenly, so there are no gaps in the sound. Give the line a sense of direction, with a minimal *crescendo* to bar 4.

The middle line (above), played by the right hand, is an important inner part, adding sonority, providing the meat on the metaphorical bones. Practice by listening to every note; they must be very even rhythmically and tonally, and fully *legato*. Aim for lighter lower notes, usually played by the thumb; the E♭, in bars 1 and 2 above, for example.

The top line (above), also played by the right hand, forms the central melody or theme, and must sing out. The third, fourth and fifth fingers will need strength and control. Practice the line alone always using the intended fingering, listening for the most important points in each phrase. It might be necessary to employ finger substitution here when creating a smooth line.

Bar 4 of the example could be considered the first 'mini-climax'. Grade the sound accordingly, aiming to *crescendo* up to bar 4; try to play with a sense of direction, avoiding a bumpy, uneven line. Hand flexibility will be vital, as some of the intervals may be considered large for the smaller hand; bar 1, beat 2, to bar 2, beat 1 and bar 3, beat 2 (second eighth note) to bar 4, beat 1, for example. Keep the hand relaxed and join notes with the fingers as much as possible.

Plenty of separate work on each layer will make the eventual combination feel more comfortable.

Key: A♭ major
Time signature: $\frac{2}{4}$
Tempo: Adagio *Cantabile*: ♪ = 66
Style: Classical
Technical Focus: *Legato, cantabile* line, balancing layers of sound, and warm sonority.

PRACTICE TECHNIQUE

Right-hand practice

Ensure ornamental passages are even, for example, bar 13, beat 2; resist the temptation to rush, placing notes carefully with a light touch, thinking of them as part of the melodic line.

Try counting the whole movement in sixteenth notes and keep a very even pulse. Paired sixteenth notes should be played with a slow drop-roll technique. An interesting Eighteenth century performance practice detail is that *staccato* notes under slurs (as at bar 15, beat 2), can sometimes mean pulling back the tempo, especially if approaching a cadence.

The dramatic middle section (bars 37–50), will require control. As with the layers at the beginning, work at the top line alone, harbouring strength and a deep sound. The lower chords must all sound together, and be articulated lightly. You may need to change hand positions swiftly to manage each beat rhythmically, as at bars 40–41, for example.

As the theme returns (bar 51), the lower accompaniment demands accurate articulation. Slur the first two notes, but keep repeated notes light.

Left-hand practice

The left-hand sixteenth-note passages from bars 9–22, should ideally be soft and light, rhythmically supporting the right hand, but also using a skimming technique free from any bumps or jerkiness. Ensure the lower line of the left hand is as smooth as possible (bars 9–11). Chords should be balanced and depressed altogether, especially during the climax in the middle section (bars 42–43) and at the end (bars 67 and 69).

The left-hand answering phrase at bars 38–41, will need a specific phrasing; *staccato* within a *legato* phrase might be best interpreted with a soft *non-legato* touch.

Hands together

At bars 9–10, there are four musical lines; aim to think of them as soprano, alto, tenor and bass. They may be practiced separately or together in various guises. The significant outer parts are marked:

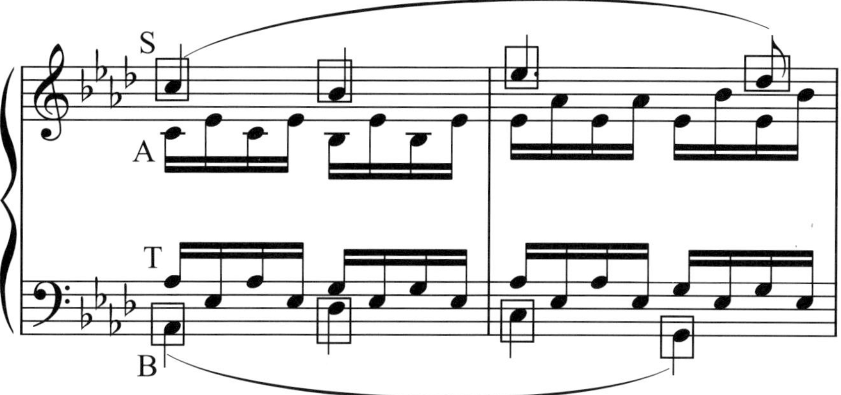

When you combine all four, the part playing should feel comfortable, allowing for greater tonal control of each part.

INTERPRETATION

Mark the top of each phrase, so you are clear about phrase structure; the success of this movement relies on waves and peaks of sound. Explore as many soft sonorities as possible and ensure longer melody notes; for example, the quarter and dotted quarter notes in bars 1 and 2 of the right hand, employ substantial arm-weight, so that their sound carries over to the next note.

Turns (at bars 20 and 21) and *acciaccaturas* (bars 70–72) must be graceful and eloquent, forming part of the melodic line.

Sforzando, *fortepiano* (loud but suddenly soft) and *rinforzando* (with a sudden increase of force) punctuate at regular intervals. They provide structure to Beethoven's sentences.

Tip

Whilst this movement is very expressive, it is an example of the Classical style, therefore keep *rubato* to a minimum, employing a *ritenuto* just at the end of a section (for example, at bar 50) and the end of the piece (bars 72–73).

Allegro
Third Movement

PREPARATION

The third movement is a Rondo, where the main theme (bars 1–17) alternates with other contrasting thematic material. It's full of energy and passion. As it bubbles along at speed, dexterity is a prerequisite throughout, so here are a few ideas for neat and tidy articulation. Let's prepare the left hand for the Alberti bass type patterns; an accompaniment consisting of broken or arpeggiated chords. The left hand is full of such figurations and they can be challenging to control at speed. Practice in chords, moving quickly between them, so you have ample time to find the notes and fingerings:

Set up

Key: C minor
Time signature: ₵
Tempo: Allegro: 𝅗𝅥 = 108
Style: Classical
Technical Focus:
Broken chord figurations, *Alberti* bass, ornaments and fast passagework.

Bar 1 Bar 12

Now work with different rhythmic patterns, providing accents and *tenuto* markings as written:

Bar 1

Bar 12

Practice slowly, with special emphasis on the lower notes, as these offer shape to the bass line. It's advisable to keep the upper parts of any *Alberti* bass figuration, light and soft. This frequently involves thumbs, so you may find the following exercise beneficial; try to find a comfortable area on the right tip of the thumb and stick to that spot for every note, really connecting with the key:

Based on bar 12 and 13

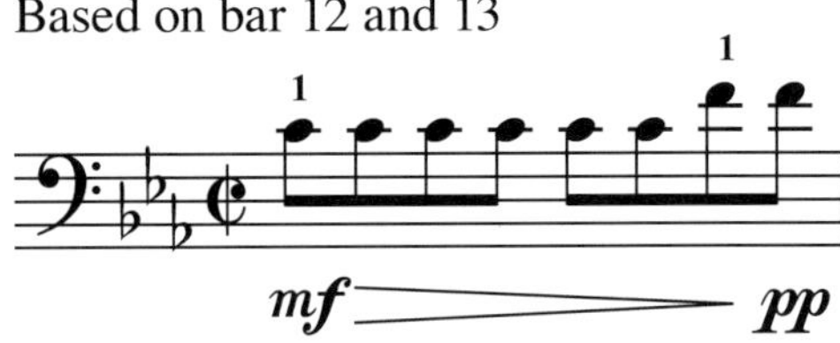

Play with a full sound, then gradually decrease your tone, until barely audible. When playing such passages at tempo, weight your hand towards the lower line and use a very quick rotational hand movement. Tension might arise if the wrist is kept in one position, therefore move frequently, releasing any stiffness, and practice in short sections.

PRACTICE TECHNIQUE

Right-hand practice

Phrasing is a vital component throughout. From the *staccato* upbeat at the opening to the rapid scale passages, each musical sentence needs a specific touch. As a general rule, *staccato* passages are best played with a brushing or stroking touch primarily using just the top of the finger (as shown in the photo) from the first finger joint, in a flicking or scratching motion, moving inwards.

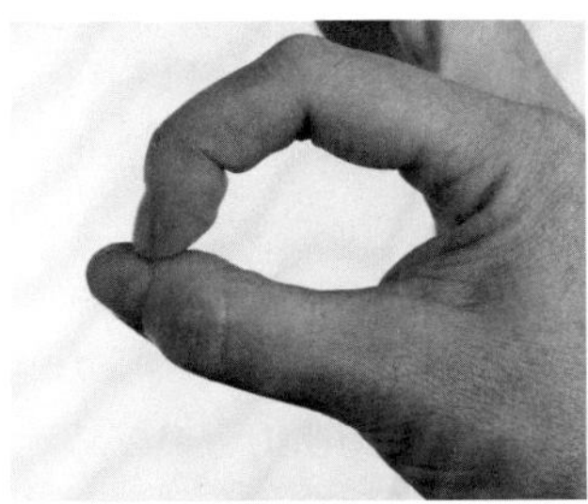

Softer passagework containing *staccato*, for example the chordal passage from bars 44–50, demands a slower paced *staccato*; lift off the keys slowly, as if *non-legato*, in keeping with the expressive style and character.

Ornaments such as the *acciaccaturas* should be played very short or 'crushed' on to the main note, as shown here in the first subject, or main theme:

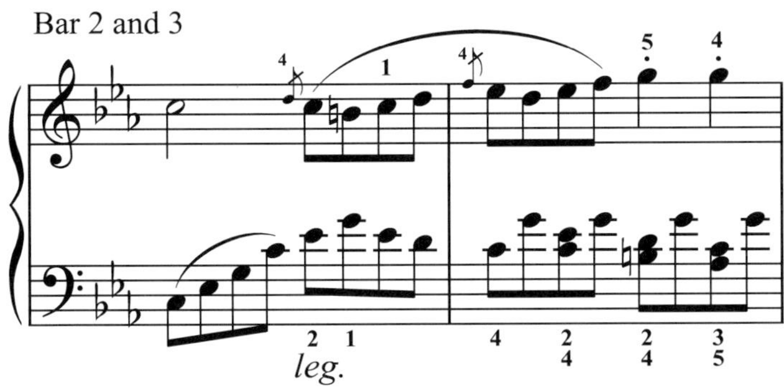

However, grace notes, such as that on the first beat of bar 5 and the trill at bar 16, should ideally be played on the beat, every note clearly sounding. Close articulation and active finger tips will be necessary to achieve this.

Scale figurations, like those at bars 103–106, and repeated note patterns, need precision and contouring. It's too easy for these patterns to be uneven and 'swallowed' at speed. When working slowly, find points within each passage to focus on, for example, at bar 189 and similar places. Here the fourth finger requires attention, in order to hold the pulse:

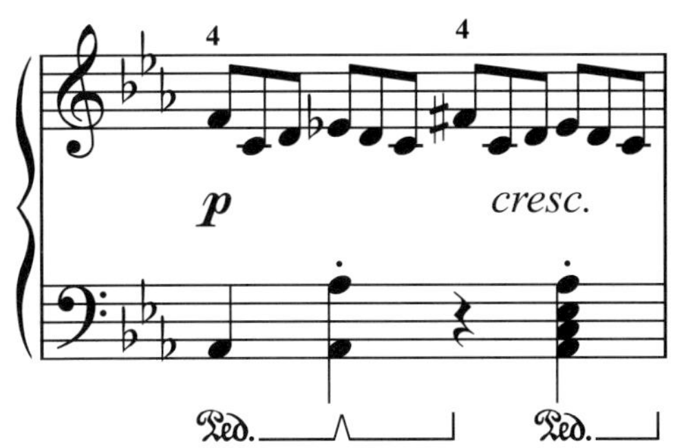

Accents and slow heavy work will help, as will turning the hand and wrist to the right, away from the body, to support the fourth finger. When using the fourth finger in this passage, make sure it has a solid connection to the key, using the tips of the fingers with no collapsing joints, and aim for a deep touch in order to avoid rushing. The E♭ eighth note (at the beginning of the triplet figure on beat 2 and 4 of the bar), might also benefit from a similar firm approach.

Broken Chords

Bar 19, and many similar passages in this piece, will benefit from the following practice tool. Play altogether, with intended fingering, as in bar 1 of the example:

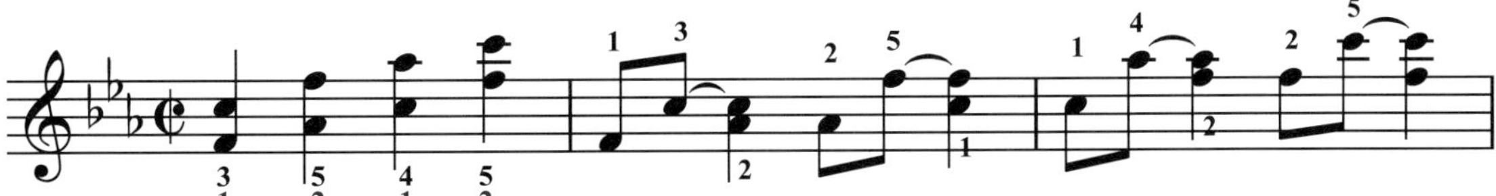

When working at the 'joins' in between each note group, make a circular motion with your wrist, leaving the second quarter note (in bar 1 of the example) quickly, to rotate onto the third quarter note. Bars 2 and 3 (of the example above) offer further practice suggestions to develop a relaxed motion, moving between eighth notes.

This wave-like motion, using the down-up or drop-rise wrist technique, featured in the first movement, between notes, is very useful and propels the hand freely up the keyboard, guiding the fingers to the correct notes. Practice slowly, taking speed up gradually.

Left-hand practice

The left hand is a constant support to the right, and must therefore add depth and rhythmical energy. Accompanying chords which are not phrased can generally be executed using a *non-legato* technique (bars 20–24, bars 152–153, bars 209–210). Aim to give *staccato* chords more bite and a bolder attack (as at bar 185, and bars 190–198).

Tip

The left hand assumes the melody at bar 129–132; encourage the bass line to mimic the right hand's articulation, with short phrases, and a sweeping sound on the half notes.

Hands together

Coordination demands focus in this movement. Attaining even, rhythmical eighth notes could well be the greatest challenge. When practicing with both hands, thorough technical preparation will pay dividends. Set a slow pulse on the metronome, and ensure complete coordination between the right-hand's single eighth notes (which follow the dotted quater notes) and left-hand eighth notes as at bar 1. Aim to come off all ties promptly, this is also crucial for rests too.

Practice deliberately with a heavy touch, listening to every note as you coordinate such passages as at bars 98–106. Resist any urge to rush the *staccato* eighths in either hand. When secure, bring out the melodic interest, so the scale passages become background accompaniment.

Bars 107–115 could be practiced like this, based on bar 107:

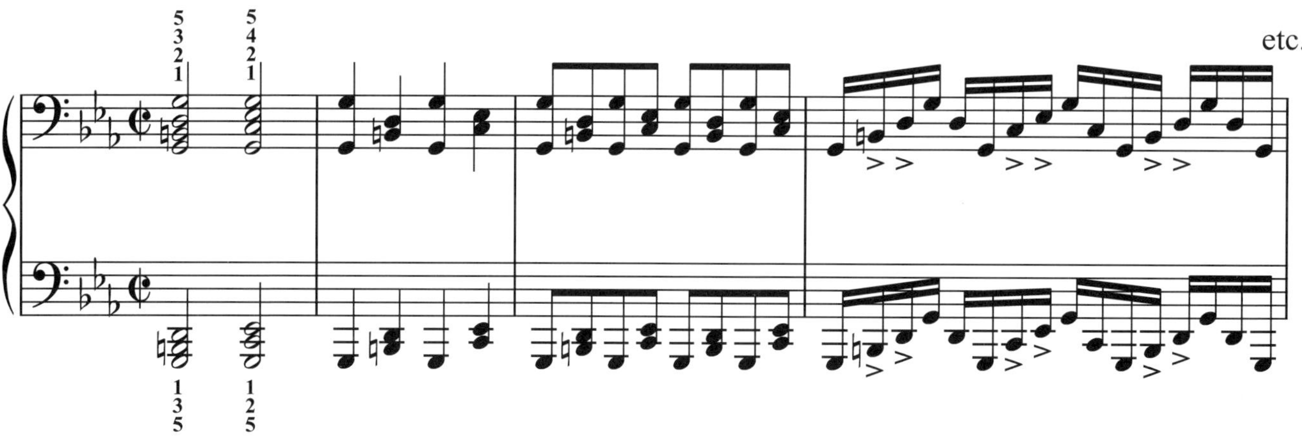

INTERPRETATION

Some pedalling has been included, but don't be tempted to over-pedal this movement. You could join much of the opening material (bars 1–17) with finger *legato*, possibly adding the smallest touches of sustaining pedal on every half-note beat. Consider pedalling held chords such as those at bars 58–61, the *szforzando* chords at bars 193–198 as well as rapid passagework as at bars 107–112.

Certain melody notes can be featured, as they punctuate the melodic sentences, as at bar 12, beats 2 and 4, for example. This is also true of chordal passages, such as those at bars 18 and 22, which announce new material.

The whole piece might benefit from mental orchestration; thinking about a Classical style work, such as this piece, in terms of orchestral instrumentation can conjure particular sounds or timbres for various musical lines, leading to a more interesting interpretation.

The choral (hymn-like) section at bars 78/79–98 (beat 1) calls for a much softer sonority; the inverted (a melody turned upside down) four-bar theme, might work well with a variety of dynamic colours. Enjoy experimenting with softer timbres, but always play this section *legatissimo*, spotlighting the first five notes of the phrase.

A thunderous penultimate bar demanding strong, agile finger work brings this masterpiece to a close.

Sonata in C minor (Pathétique)

Op. 13

Ludwig van Beethoven (1770–1827)

attacca subito
Allegro di molto e con brio
cresc.
cresc.
cresc.

37
sf
Ped.
44
sf
p
51
simile
58
65

72
79
rf
decresc.
(132)
(13)
87
(decresc.)
pp
p
Ped.
92
cresc.
simile
98
(cresc.)
f
p
Ped.
Ped.

cresc.
f
p
cresc.
simile
f
f
sf
sf
sf
ff
sf
ff
1.
2.

Tempo I
fp
decresc.
pp
attacca subito
Allegro molto e con brio
p
cresc.
f
simile

168
cresc.
173
sf
pp
178
cresc.
sf
sf
184
sf
fp
190

195
p
sf
cresc.
201
p
sf
207
cresc.
p cresc.
214
p cresc.
p
221
sf
sf
229
sf
sf

237
sf
sf
245
decresc.
pp
253
p
cresc.
258
f
264
p
cresc.
270
f

276
281
cresc.
287
sf
f cresc.
ff
ff
295
Grave
p
cresc.
sf
decresc.
pp
299
Allegro molto e con brio
p
sf
cresc.
304
ff
ff

Adagio cantabile ♪ = 66
p legato
Ped.
simile

23
cresc.
p
cresc.
27
p
pp
p
32
36
pp
Ped.
39
cresc.
Ped.
Ped.

42
sf
sf
sf
fp
decresc.
simile
45
pp
48
cresc.
51
p
55
simile

58
61
64
67
70
pp
(or 1 2 2 2 2)
rf
rf
rf
pp
Ped.
Ped.
Ped.
Ped.
Ped.

Rondo

Allegro 𝅗𝅥 = 108

33
p
sf
sf
Ped.
Ped.
simile
37
non leg.
41
p
Ped.
47
cresc.
sf
f
simile
p
53
sf
sf
cresc.
57
ff
sf
p
Ped.

62
leg.
66
Ped.
70
cresc.
74
tr
f
p
Ped.
79
p
Ped.
simile
87

95
101
cresc.
f
105
sf
cresc.
Ped.
109
simile
ff
112
sf
116
ff
sf
p
Ped.

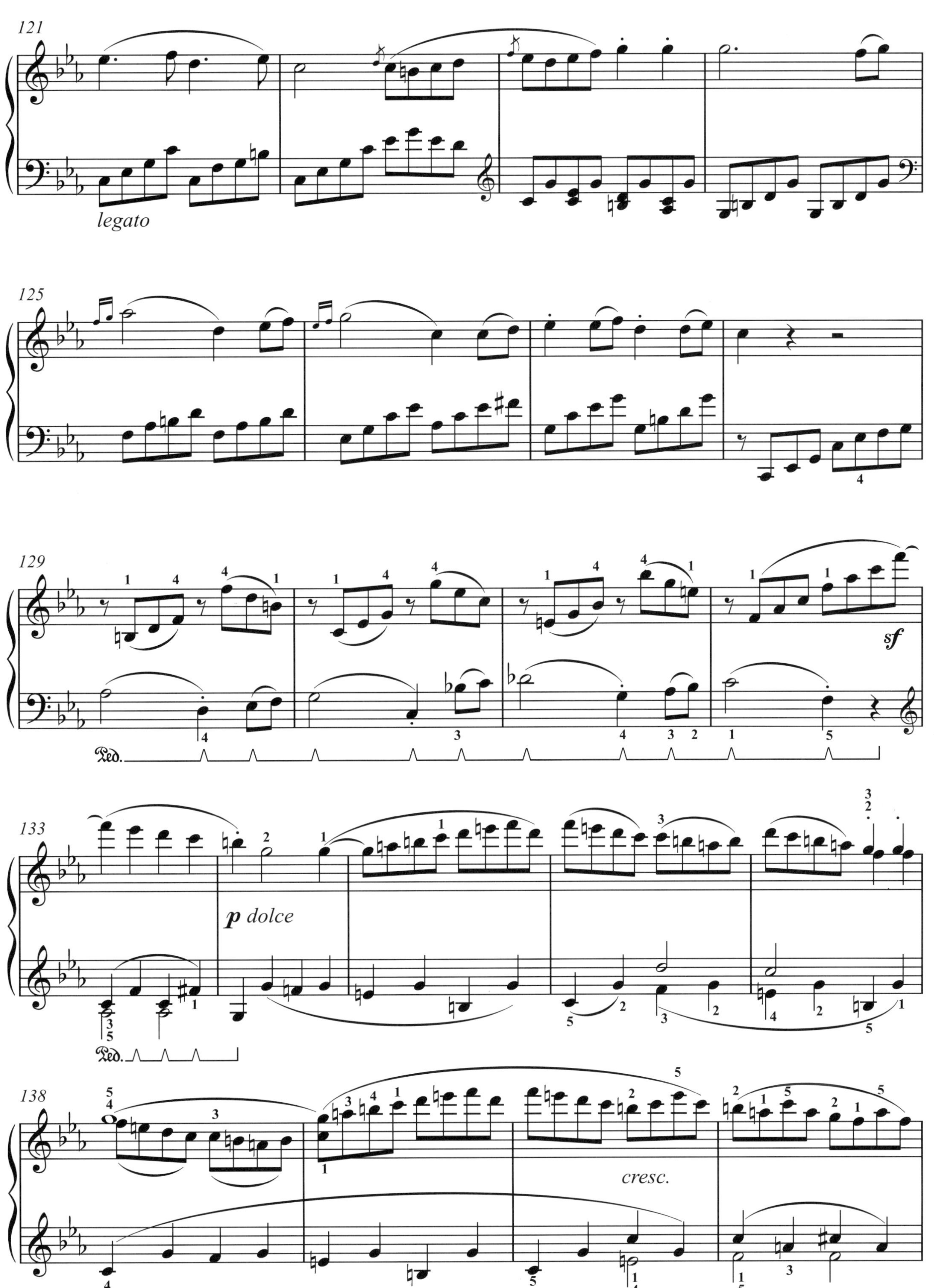

121
legato
125
129
sf
Ped.
133
p dolce
Ped.
138
cresc.

simile
simile
calando

169
(calando)
p
leg.
174
178
cresc.
182
p
cresc.
sf
sf
ff
186
sf
sf
p
cresc.

190
193
197
201
206
decresc.

Intermezzo in A major

Johannes Brahms (1833–1897)

Set up

Key: A major
Time signature: $\frac{3}{4}$
Tempo: *Andante teneramente:* ♩ = 60
Style: Romantic
Technical Focus: Chordal texture, finger substitution, smooth *legato*, balancing layers of sound, and pedal control.

The Intermezzo *is a Nineteenth century lyrical character piece. Brahms' works in this form have wide emotional range, depth and intimacy, often consisting of a thick texture and rich chromatic harmony. Composed in 1893 as part of the* Sechs Klavierstücke Op. 118, *Brahms employs a 'developing variation' technique.*

PREPARATION

For the scale and arpeggio of A major, see page 70 of Book 1. An important aspect of this work is to develop the technique of changing fingers rapidly on one and the same note; known as finger substitution, this helps to create a smooth *legato* line. The following exercise may help:

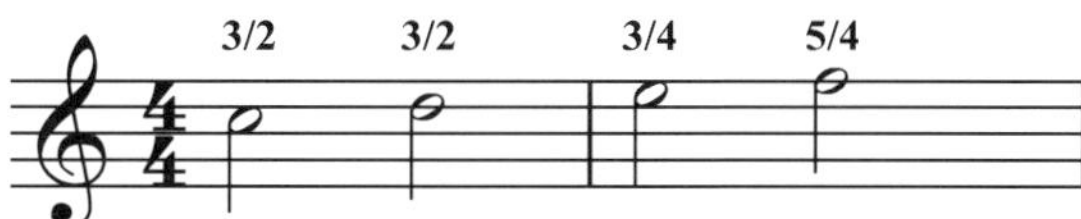

Play each note with the first fingering, and then change mid-way through the note to the second fingering. Once you have played the note with the first finger, keep it silently depressed and manoeuvre the subsequent finger into place whilst all the time holding down the key with the first. Finally, let the second finger take the weight of the note, freeing the first finger to continue the *legato* pattern. This technique encourages an unbroken *legato* musical line, and allows you to move from note to note easily changing fingers. Let's apply this principle to bars 57–60:

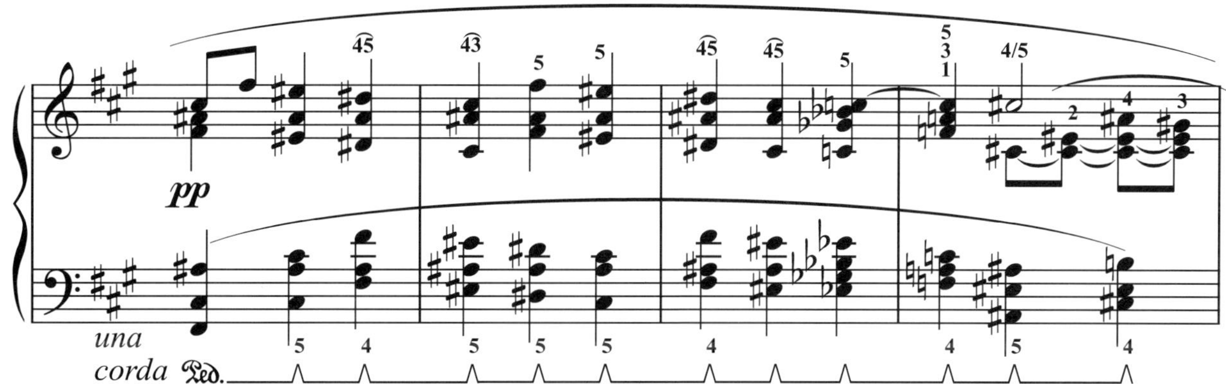

Several chords contain a finger change in the top line; this might seem challenging at first, but with slow repetitive work, it will eventually feel natural. Add the chords underneath softly. Flexibility in the hand, specifically around the fourth and fifth fingers, will be helpful.

PRACTICE TECHNIQUES

Right-hand practice

A thick texture, with assorted chordal changes and some contrapuntal passagework, demands slow assimilation with attention to fingering and note patterns. The top of octaves or chords must be free to 'sing out'; larger intervals such as a fourth, fifth and sixth, appear in the melody at bars 69, 72, 78, 79 and 80, and will require a relaxed hand and colour on the top note.

When focusing on creating *legato*, it may be necessary to slightly overlap fingers, ensuring complete transfer of weight from one note to the next; this is all connected to a fluid sound. The overlap time when one finger plays a fraction before releasing the previous finger will be extremely small, probably a minuscule of a second, but it will help avoid any clipped phrases.

Fluid Sound

Expressivity in the melodic line will benefit from a deeper touch, yet this piece stops short of the brighter *cantabile* style required in much Romantic repertoire. The intimate character of Brahms' music needs a softer, understated, mellow, muted tonal quality. To achieve this, let's take the first phrase (bars 1–4), which illustrates the main theme, as an example:

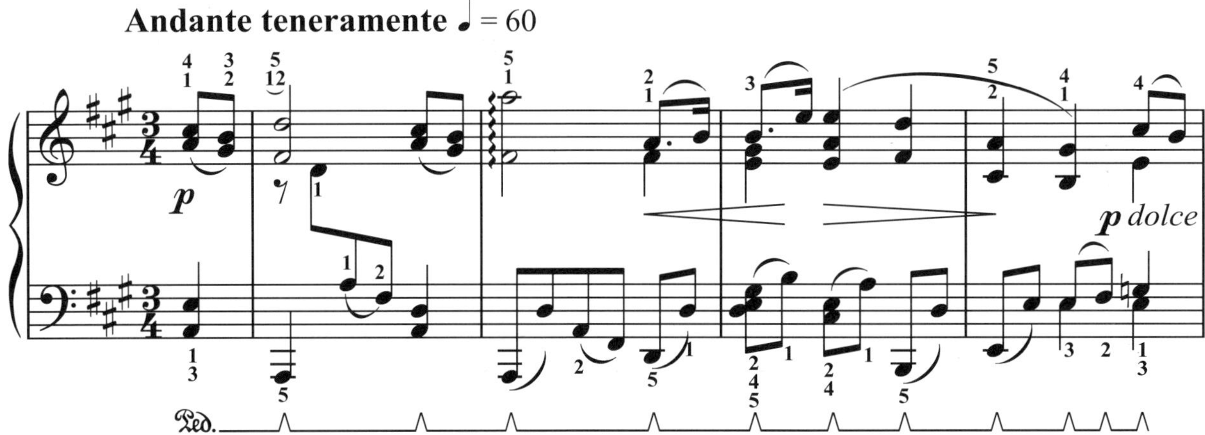

It might be useful to work at each note group as has been discussed in the technical tips on double notes on page 42. Try to keep a smooth melodic line by skimming the keys lightly without 'landing' heavily on any one note or chord. Use the following exercises for the top line. For practice purposes, employ a **very** heavy touch at first, using your fingertips incorporating arm-weight. Accent the main beats with the fingering to be played when negotiating both parts:

Now change the accents, with more sound on the less important notes; this is to test listening skills and practice a firmer touch. Hopefully fingers now feel stronger and in control. Aim to play the whole passage as soft *(ppp)* as you dare, remembering that the notes must still sound; the slower your 'attack', the softer the sound.

Attune your ears carefully in order to interpret the following passage. All notes must be graded, as suggested in the markings. Phrase off the last two quarter notes (crotchets) and resist using too much *rubato*:

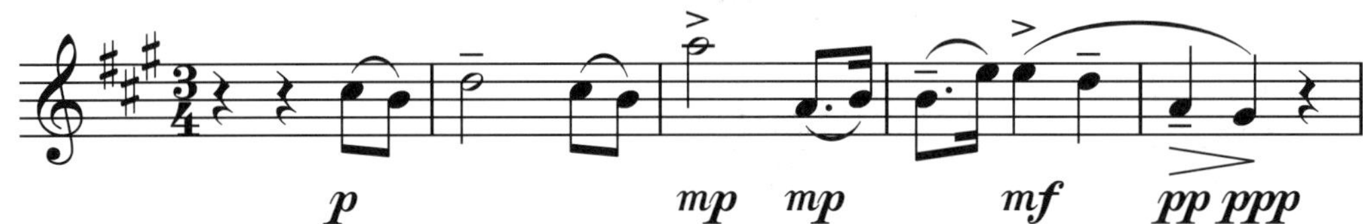

The *tenuto* markings and accents are for guidance only, and are akin to a leaning or nuancing, as opposed to an accentuation.

When you put the top melody line with the lower line, your hand and arm should ideally be weighted towards the outer part of the hand for support. The addition of arm-weight will allow the sound to carry and penetrate through the texture, yet if you now apply slightly flatter fingers with a pliable wrist, it will be softer and more muted. The angle at which you approach the keys will make a difference to the sound, therefore observe your movements. The lower right-hand line can be light, shadowing the melody.

Left-hand practice
Brahms is renowned for writing heavily textured bass lines. Much of his music uses low pitches. This adds depth and expressivity. Work at the left hand bar by bar, and note by note, taking into account each often widespread movement. For practice purposes abstain from the sustaining pedal, so you can hear and assess *legato* playing.

When practicing the bass line, decide which notes are of importance and give them more colour, providing definition, as marked in this passage (bars 43–45), highlighted with box circles:

Some bass notes need holding for entire beats. Where this isn't possible, unless you have a large hand, such as at bars 38–41, the sustaining pedal can be employed:

Figurations at bars 49–50 call for a flexible hand, often combined with a lateral wrist movement, so you can cover the keyboard and play all intervals comfortably; the fingers quickly turning over the hand for a *legato* line.

Hold the top notes, marked with box circles in the example, which are *staccato* under a slur, therefore use the thumb and second finger to gently 'feed' the notes into the texture as a countermelody to the right hand line:

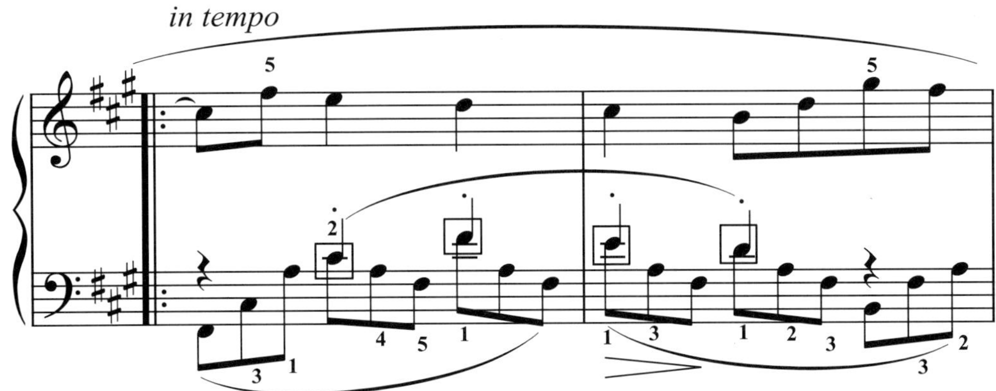

Large chords at bars 34 and 35 (and 102 and 103) might be spread or distributed, as suggested in this adjacent example, for those with smaller hands:

Some may prefer to play the chord in the second bar of the example, before the beat, with the top E on the beat. Occasionally, fingers won't be able to join notes, unless you have a larger hand, and the illusion of *legato* comes into play, as in the left hand of the adjacent example (bar 41):

If you decide to use the fingering in brackets, lightly brush each note, feeding it into the texture, but without accenting. The use of the sustaining pedal will ensure *legato*.

From bar 65, Brahms offers a captivating inner part, which interweaves with the right-hand thematic material, for highly expressive counterpoint. The voicing of the middle line (E, D, and C♯ quarter notes, in the example), commands a sonorous touch:

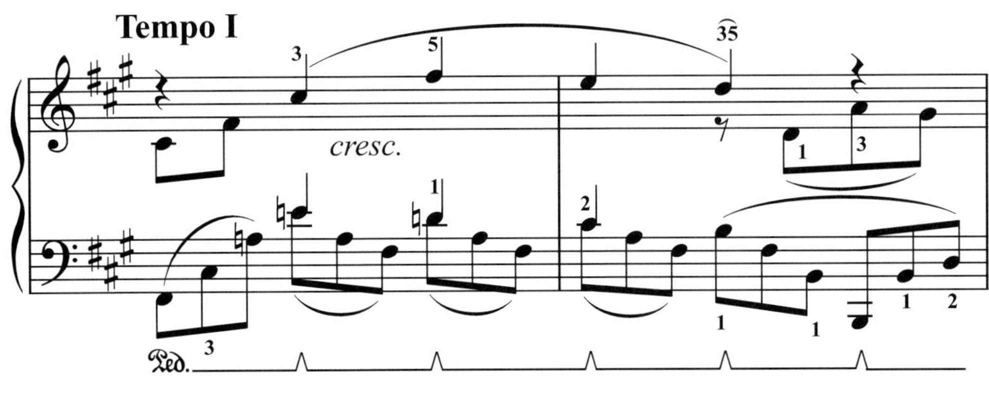

Chordal Movement

Once notes are secure, take each four-bar phrase and block out the chordal shapes. This won't always be possible due to the large intervals, but working this way encourages good coordination. Some patterns require sudden contrary movement; by practicing altogether, you will understand when and how to gauge these movements, so you can cope with ease. If we examine this passage (bars 7 and 8):

It might be practiced like this:

Work bar by bar, then phrase by phrase in this manner. Spend time on the movements which feel uncomfortable; in bar 7 this might include the jump in the right hand from beat 2 to beat 3. Play the first chord with a large sound, moving quickly with a relaxed hand to play the F♯, D♯ and A; it can help to work at the top two notes alone, gauging the jump. Playing passages at several speeds, especially at double speed, will really pay dividends.

Hands together
Syncopated rhythms, such as those at bars 31–34 in the left hand need a very soft touch, so the notes are barely audible. The frequent polyrhythmic passages, duplets against triplets, might be practiced as suggested on pages 39/40, but in this style, they can have a slightly relaxed feel, and, as always, with the melody taking precedence.

Tip

Work through the entire piece with the metronome using a slow eighth note (quaver) pulse, so you can grasp the structure and musical line. Next, practice up to speed; it can help to practice at faster tempi than that marked too, for securing note patterns. After a while you can relax the pulse and employ subtle *rubato*, paying attention to Brahms's precise tempo markings; particularly *ritenuto* (bars 45, 56, 60, 63, 74 and 113), *piu lento* (bars 46/7, 57, and 114), *calando* (gradually decreasing in speed and volume) at bars 33/34 and 101, and *un poco animato* at bars 39 and 107.

INTERPRETATION

Aim to observe all phrase marks. *Crescendo* markings should be carefully adhered to; they nearly always emphasise the top of the phrase.

Pedalling has been marked throughout, and whilst only a suggestion, the success of the sustaining pedal depends on the combination of ear and foot. Some phrases will need flutter or half pedalling, in order to lose non-harmony notes but still catch bass notes. The *una corda* (left pedal) adds serenity and a different, more muted timbre to the chorale (hymn-like) section from bars 57–64. This passage contains an ethereal quality and might be more convenient to play with flatter fingers and a slower, gentle depression of the keys.

Several tempo changes can only be implemented effectively after rhythmic practice, and there must be a cohesive sense of structure despite this work being a relaxed Intermezzo; the constantly developing thematic motifs and emotional urgency only come to life with an onward moving pulse.

Tip

Pauses or fermatas offer crucial breathing space at bars 64 and 76 (and at the end, bar 116); they can afford to be held slightly longer than strictly necessary for dramatic effect.

Intermezzo in A major

Op. 118 No. 2

Johannes Brahms (1833–1897)

legato
cresc.
espr.
calando
p dim.
dolce
cresc. un poco animato
rit.
più lento

in tempo
rit.
più lento
rit.
Tempo I
una corda
tre corde
espr.
cresc.
dim.

rit.
in tempo
p
dolce
pp
sf
dolce
espr.
cresc.
legato

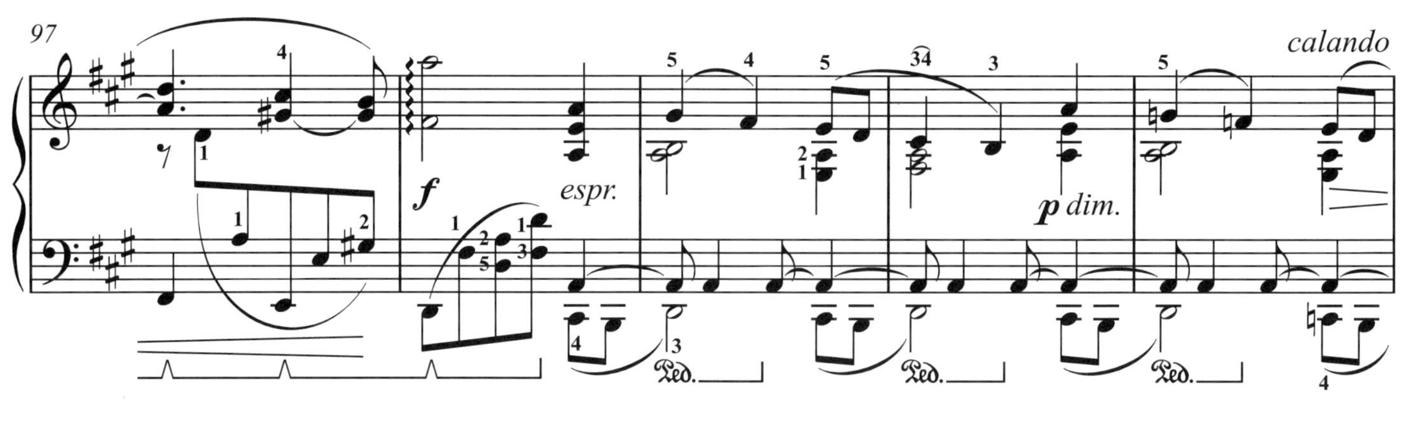
97
calando
espr.
p dim.

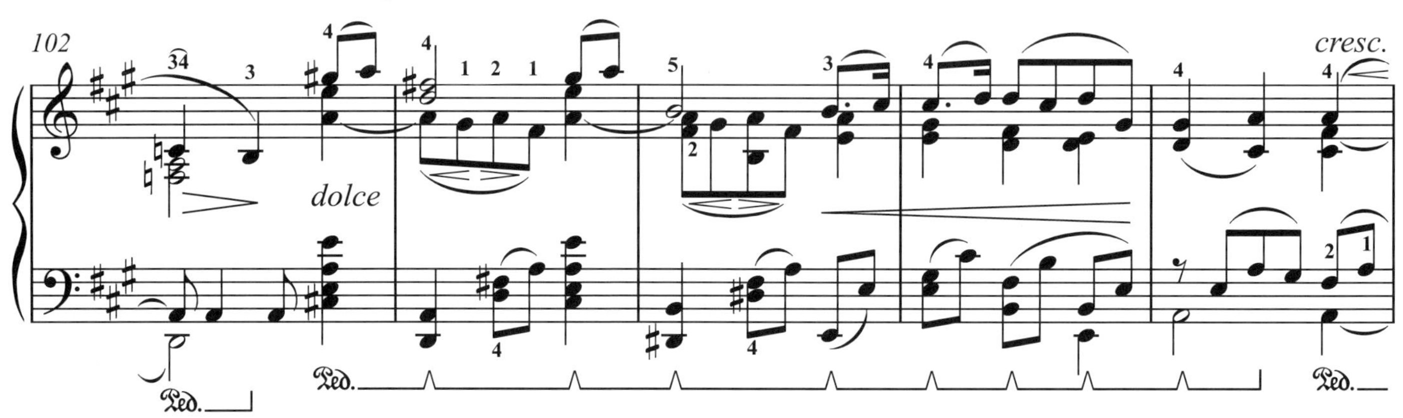
102
cresc.
dolce

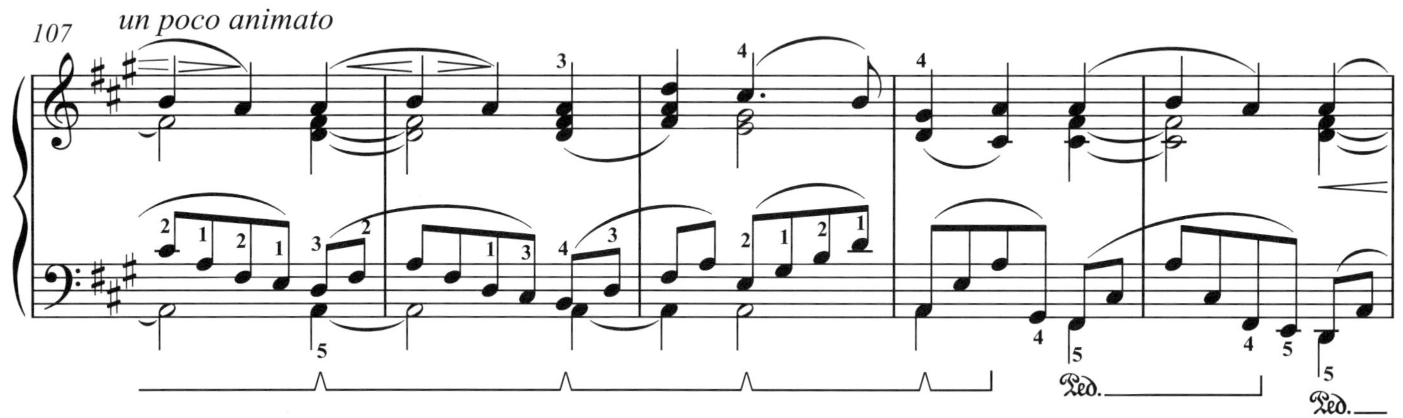
107
un poco animato

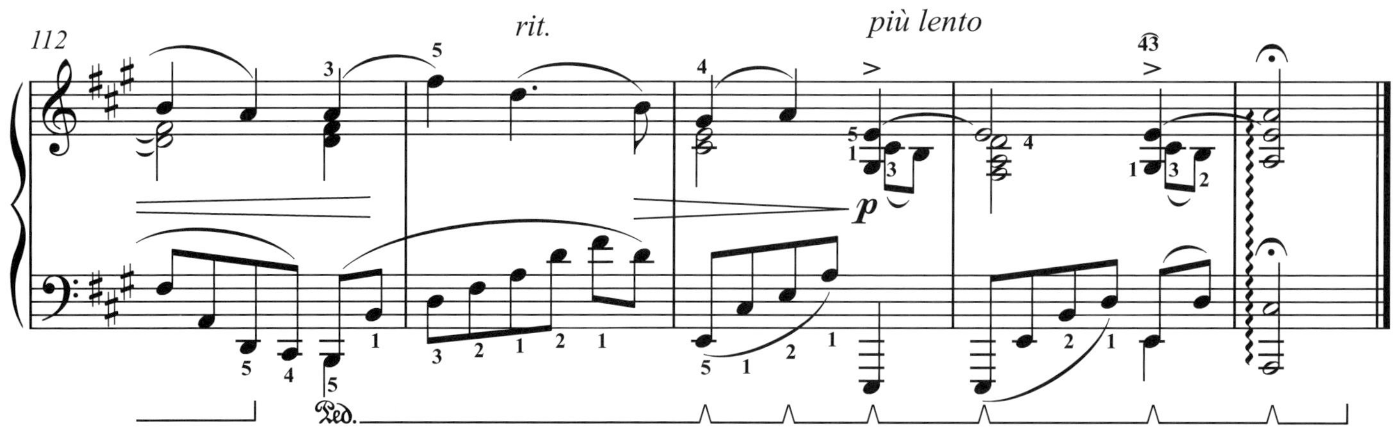
112
rit.
più lento

Wilde Jagd

Edward MacDowell (1860–1908)

Set up

Key: C♯ minor
Time signature: 6/8
Tempo: *Allegro furioso:* ♩. = 108–116
Style: Romantic
Technical Focus:
A light touch, wrist *staccato*, even sixteenth notes (semi-quaver) passages, and powerful, resonant chords.

Wilde Jagd *means 'Wild Chase', which is exactly the character this imaginative study exudes. American composer Edward MacDowell's set of* Twelve Virtuoso Studies Op. 46 *are largely programmatic. Written in Ternary form, it demands neat staccato and a powerful sound. The work concludes with an impressive coda.*

PREPARATION

The scale and arpeggio of C♯ minor can be found in Book 2 on page 49. A study has been featured in every level of this piano course, and the inclusion of this present one is designed to further develop technical grasp. For our preparation exercise, let's work on one of the most important technical issues: wrist *staccato*.

Wrist Staccato

The opening chordal passage (bars 1 and 2) requires wrist *staccato*.

1 Start by learning the note patterns slowly, observing the fingering, working at the note figurations both separately and hands together. Different physical movements will be necessary depending on your practice speed, therefore work at slow and faster tempi successively.

2 A 'fluttering' technique in the wrists can be helpful in order to obtain the correct movement and physical feeling of wrist *staccato*. Away from the keyboard, move your wrists rapidly in an up-and-down or hinge-like motion. Arms should remain fairly still, hand movements being controlled by the wrist. This should feel comfortable, light and relaxed with no tension. Begin slowly, working up to fast speeds; see photos below which show the first chord being struck and its subsequent release in bar 1.

1

2

3

3 Wrist *staccato* can be achieved by 'bouncing' off the notes; move off the first chord quickly (photo 1), with an upward motion from the wrist, as seen in the second and third photo, then a downward movement catching the subsequent chord. Practice this pattern at slow speeds, observing your wrists, encouraging them to bounce up and down with a loose, flexible motion between each chord.

4 At speed, this movement will become almost imperceptible, but continuous wrist movement will help to alleviate any possible tension, and it will also assist in providing a light, detached character.

5 When playing extended chordal passages employing *staccato*, a rising and falling wrist motion in between sections will help banish tension. To do this play a series of chords, for example, at bars 31–34, and find a suitable gap, perhaps every two bars, to allow the wrists to rise more than usual, falling on the first beat of the next two-bar phrase, 'placing' the first chord of each new two-bar section:

Aim to do this consciously at first, releasing the muscles and tendons in the wrist and hand completely within each 'gap' or break; after a while this will become a habit. This is similar to implementing 'gaps' or tension breaks as discussed during other repertoire in this book; the drop-rise motion is a vital technique when playing any extended passage which could potentially tense the arm, hand and wrist.

PRACTICE TECHNIQUES

Right-hand practice

Sixteenth note passages such as those at bars 3, 4, 47 and 48, need strong fingers. Try the following example slowly, observing your movements and feeling the larger intervals via a relaxed flexible hand:

These extended finger patterns will focus your attention on the fourth and fifth fingers. Add accents and a deeper touch both at slow and fast speeds, moving the wrist and arm at appropriate places when practicing.

The movement from bar 3 beat 1 to beat 2 must be a quick but flexible manoeuvre, as the fourth finger turns over the fifth; from the F♯ to G♯. Once even and rhythmical, add speed and a light touch.

Fast octave passages also need a light touch using wrist *staccato*, and when articulated at a lower position on the keyboard, such as at bars 15 and 16, move the upper torso sufficiently to the left, in order to accommodate octave positions. Chordal passages like those at bars 9, 10, 27 and 28 reveal a melody line (as marked by circles in the following example). Add colour and depth to the top line by practicing separately, keeping the lower notes in these chords very soft:

Tip

Leggiero implies a soft, will-o'-the-wisp-like delicacy, frequently occurring in the high right-hand phrases. *Wilde Jagd* combines light passagework alongside rich, ringing chords, and it's this constant oscillation which can prove challenging.

Accent the first chord in the following example, and turn the hand swiftly to support the fifth finger, remembering the door knob image, with a rapidly 'shaking' wrist (bars 51 and 52):

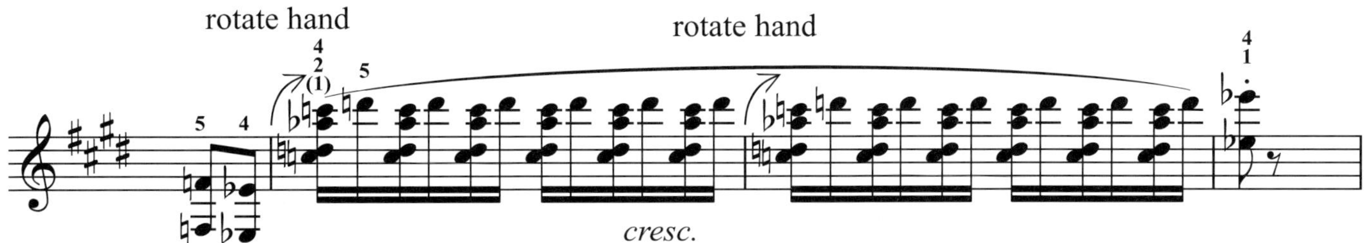

Large intervals, as at bars 96–100 can be spread, the lower notes played quickly before the main beat. Take time to place each chord, heeding the *molto allargando* instruction.

Left-hand practice

Passagework similar to trills are a feature in the left hand. These might require spot practice on specific finger movements. Examining bar 7, here are a few practice ideas, which may help to develop more control in the third and fourth fingers:

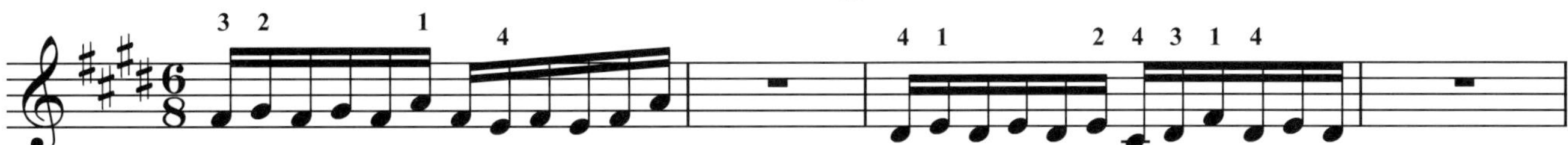

Accents and a heavy articulation are important; add your own to the example, and try to develop and even touch when articulating lightly and up to speed.

Be sure of the fingering at bars 33–34 and 37–40; a *leggiero, staccato* touch will define this section conveying the playful spirit. Aim for crisp finger work and rhythmic articulation.

As the texture changes, octave passages need definition, particularly from bars 51–57, and all similar.

Hands together

Coordination is key, especially during the interplay between the right and left hand (bar 23):

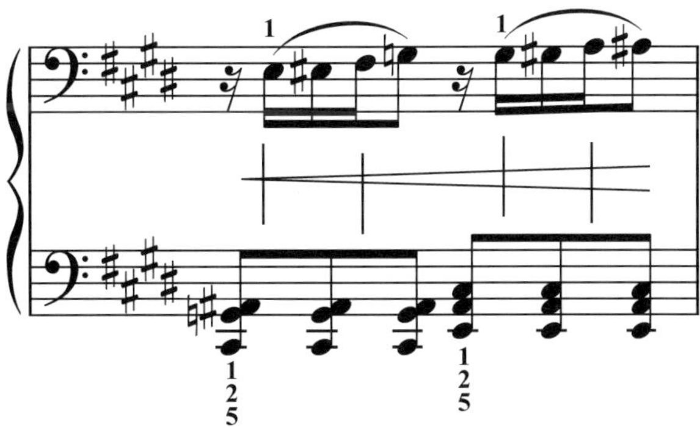

Nothing can beat slow practice. Experiment with metronome markings such as an eighth note (quaver) equals 60 beats per minute; I would practice in sixteenth notes at first, deliberately placing each note to every tick of the metronome.

The middle section, from bar 61 moving to the climax at bar 100, features hand crossing, the left hand sounding thematic material over right-hand chords. The right-hand chords can be light and supportive, but make sure the hand and wrists don't become stiff with the copious repeated chord patterns; right-hand rests on the first beat of each dotted quarter-note (dotted crotchet) beat provide the perfect place to release tension (bars 66 and 67):

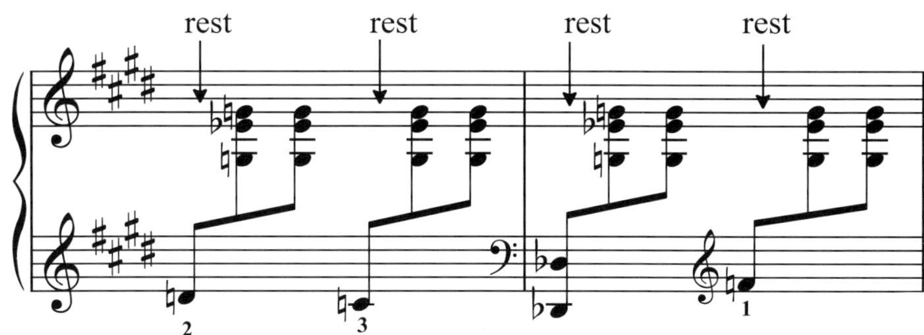

For practice purposes, try extending the left-hand pattern by jumping an octave or two further than written. The *acciaccaturas* can generally be played before the beat, in the thematic material as at bar 72:

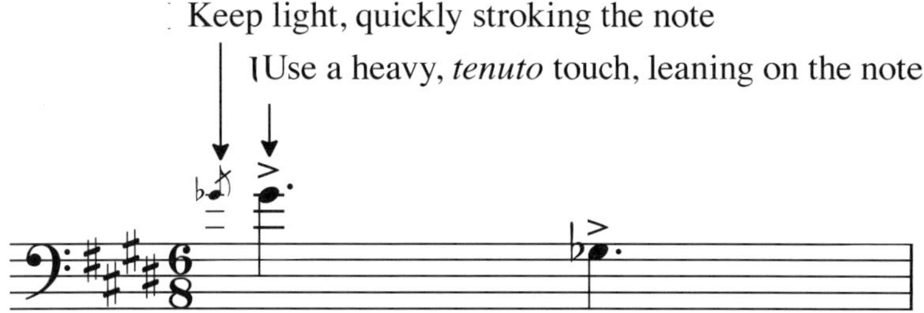

The monumental chords from bar 85 heralded by a time signature change and a distinctly march-like feel, can be placed with a gradual *ritenuto* towards bar 100. The top Gs ring out above the texture, but don't ignore the lower parts which continue the rhythmical march character (bars 85–88):

The coda from bar 127 offers a chance to circumnavigate the keyboard. To secure note patterns, here are some practice ideas based on bars 127–128:

INTERPRETATION

Rhythmic energy and accents are the life blood of this work; try to give a rhythmic push on every dotted-quarter-note beat.

Pedalling has been suggested; in this style the sustain pedal will contribute a rich sonority. Swift touches of pedal are sufficient during the outer sections, as in bars 1–24, although these bars might feasibly be played with none at all. Bars 25–26 could be effective with as much as two pedal changes per bar (on each dotted quarter note beat), and this might be considered for bars 41–42, 45–46, and 49–50 too. One pedal per bar could suffice for bars 53–56. The middle section needs more resonance to hold bass notes, as marked from bars 61–84, and the coda requires the same approach.

After the drama of the *Presto*, the final chord might be very soft, and played with a short, sharp *staccato* articulation.

Tip

Chromatic chordal passages will benefit from rhythmic vitality and dynamic sweeps of colour; MacDowell is specific with the dynamics, insisting on *fff* to *ppp* often in short spaces of time, therefore practice quick changes.

Wilde Jagd

Op. 46 No. 3

Edward MacDowell (1860–1908)

21
pp
25
p
cresc.
ten.
poco marc.
29
p
ten.
poco marc.
33
p
mf
marc.
ten.
37
fz
41
mf
marc.
ten.
fz

45
marc.
f
p subito
Ped.
48
f
Ped.
51
cresc.
Ped.
54
cresc.
cresc.
ten.
ff
furioso
ten.
58
ff
Ped.
61
poco a poco cresc.
fz
pp subito
Ped.

65
sempre poco a poco cresc.
ten.
marc.
70
sempre cresc.
ten.
ten.
75
sempre cresc.
sempre più
marcato
sim.
80
molto cresc.
85
fff
e marcatiss.
Ped.

93
sempre fff
molto allarg.
Tempo I
101
fz ff ma legg.
105
f
109
poco marc.
ff
dim.
113
f
dim.

117
mf
dim.
121
p
dim.
pp
ppp
Presto
127
pp
p
Ped.
132
8
mf
137
8
f
8
ff

Asturias Leyenda

Isaac Albeniz (1860–1909)

This ominous, pulsating work evokes pure Spanish Flamenco dance, with the well-known theme imitating the guitar technique of alternating the right hand playing the melody with the index finger sounding the repeated notes. In Ternary form, with more than a passing reference to the Phrygian mode, the incessant rhythmic pulse is akin to a strumming guitar and a Flamenco dancer's footwork.

Set up

Key: G minor
Time signature: 3/4
Tempo: *Allegro:* ♩ = 138
Style: Post Romantic
Technical Focus:
Repeated notes, large leaps, quick movement, and evenness.

PREPARATION

For the key of G minor, return to Book 1, page 23. The middle section of this piece is like a Spanish *copia* which is a type of sung verse, whereby melodic inflections resemble speech patterns, with a more relaxed feel. Start by taking each rhetoric phrase, adding dynamic nuances. Consider a *crescendo* at bar 63 then a *diminuendo* to bar 66, to match bars 67–70. Add a *tenuto* mark to the top notes, playing the *mordent* as shown, though in a rhythmically relaxed way:

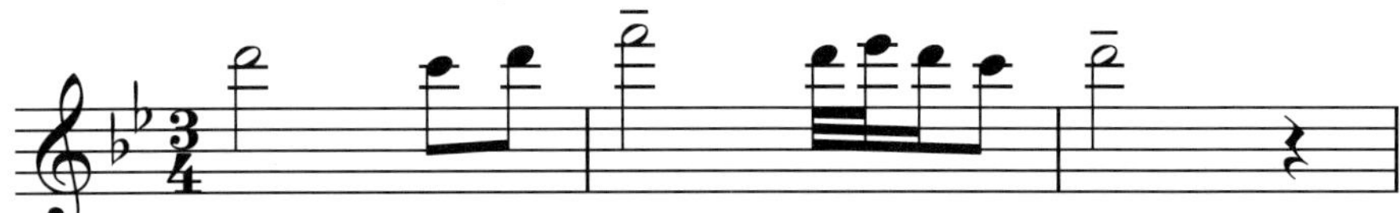

The next eight bars develop the previous passage, so you can relish the rich harmonic inflections:

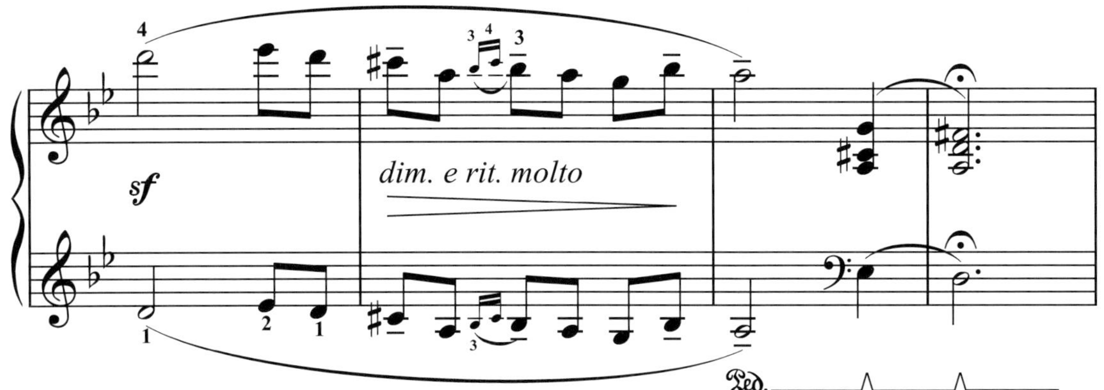

Use a deeper touch for harmonic twists, slightly lingering in both hands as shown with *tenuto* marks in the example. Hold the left-hand single notes in the brief hymn-like section from bars 79–86, keeping a very smooth *legato* line. A considered interpretation of this section is key to a sympathetic performance, hence time spent working at the melodic nuances before and during note learning will certainly be worthwile.

PRACTICE TECHNIQUES

Right-hand practice

Repeated notes are a recurrent feature. Let's begin with a few practice exercises.

The repeated right-hand Ds must be light and soft; the first bar of the example below offers an alternative fingering to that written in the score. Whilst the second finger might be the most economical way of achieving a regular repetition, it can be helpful to experiment at various speeds with assorted finger changes:

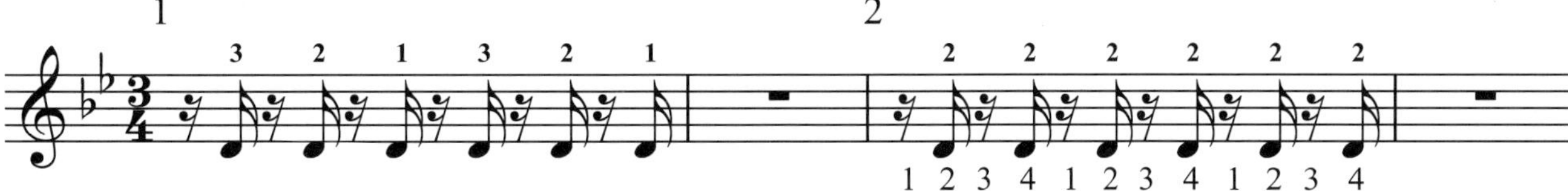

Try practicing with several tempi. The following metronome marks may be useful: start with sixteenth note (semiquaver) equals 96 beats per minute, then move to 132 and, finally, 176.

Use a quick inward movement with the top of the finger. Now replace the different finger changes with the second finger, and repeat the exercise (No. 2). Pay attention to the quality of each *staccato* note; it must be very short but not too spikey, more like a quick 'murmur' or heartbeat. Each note should ideally be exactly the same length producing an even wash of sound. Keep the second finger close to the key surface; this repeated pattern necessitates half-key or surface-key playing, where the notes don't rebound fully.

Moving to bars 17–48, the Ds are now in octaves, requiring a tension-free technique. Short breaks between each octave provide the opportunity to loosen the hand and wrist. Work at the octave passages with a very flexible wrist, keeping the octave shape and compliant finger positions, finding appropriate moments in the score to rest. When up to tempo, move the wrist and arm in an 'up-down' motion first at the end of every bar (as marked in the example below), and then after every four bar phrase. When practicing the octaves, gently depress them with a quick downward wrist movement, and afterwards, as you release the key, also aim to release any effort or tension in your upper torso instantaneously. It's this swift 'letting-go' after every octave, and then a larger release after every four bars, which will be paramount for a tension free performance:

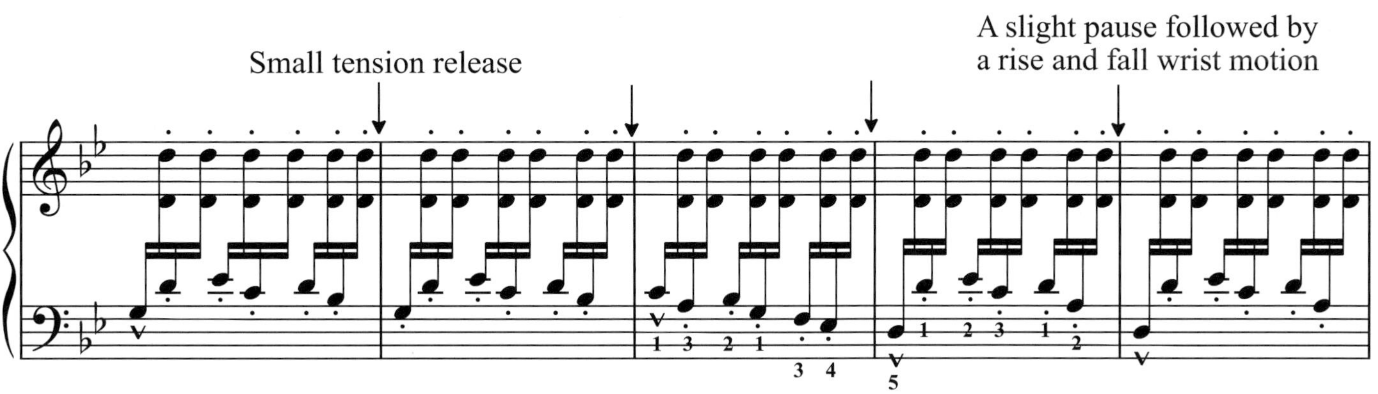

Left-hand practice
Apply right-hand practice suggestions to the left, shaping each four-bar phrase. The opening material might be phrased as follows, with more colour on notes with *tenuto* marks:

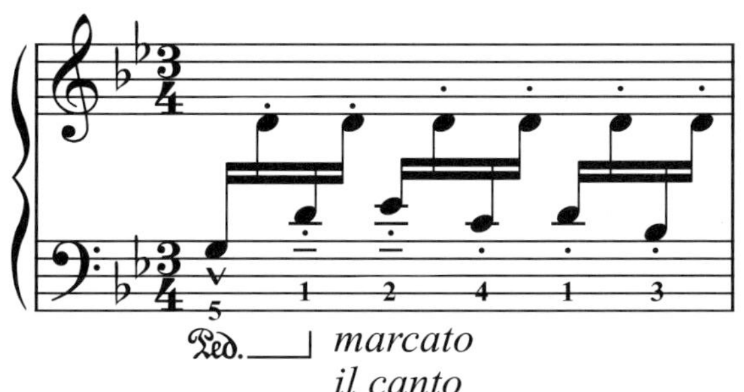

Find the climatic point in each phrase, and try to mark the accented bass notes such as those at the beginning of bars 1, 5, 6, etc. A prompt but deep touch, usually with the fifth finger will add extra timbre.

Hands together
The main technical challenge in this piece are the recurring rapid leaps; bars 25–45 and 147–167. Here are a few practice suggestions:

Quick Leaps

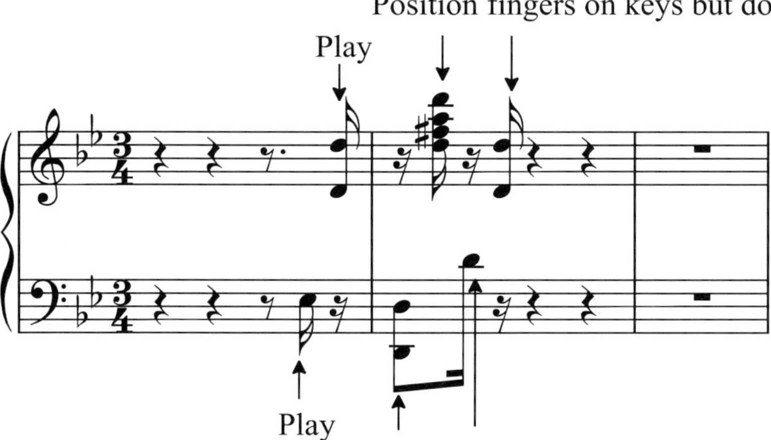

1. With separate hands, play notes before the leap moving to the following chord or octave as quickly as possible, but without sounding them:
2. Now practice the leap in the example, sounding all the notes, both hands together.
3. As you leap, focus on one hand only; keep your eyes on the right-hand jump, even though you will still play the left-hand octave, and then vice versa. This will help playing 'blind' relying on your feeling (or muscle memory) as opposed to watching the jumps. Then go one step further and practice the leaps with your eyes closed.
4. As you move, change hand shapes rapidly, in preparation for the next chord or octave.
5. Practice in small sections, even one beat at a time, thinking through the jumps; plan and synchronise them in your mind before moving, judging the distances carefully.
6. Practice both slowly and at full speed during the same practice session. The movements will be different. Keep the arms and elbows light, and fully engaged to enable swift access to the jumps. As always, release physical tension as much as possible after every leap.
7. Finally, stagger the jumps as written and take a very slight hiatus after each one, allowing the fingers and your mind to shift back to the pre-jump position, placing the notes.

INTERPRETATION
Pedalling has been suggested. A dry sound is most effective for the outer sections, in order to imitate a guitar; note repetitions can otherwise become a blur of sound. The middle section may be pedalled more freely, although quick 'dabs' will be ample for passages such as that at bars 92–94. Don't ignore the *fff* dynamics, they add intensity and contour.

Tip

The pauses or fermatas form an intrinsic part of this Spanish style. As in speech, a generous break between passages in bars 66–67, 86–87 and 105–106, will make all the difference.

Asturias Leyenda

Op. 47 No. 5

Isaac Albeniz (1860–1909)

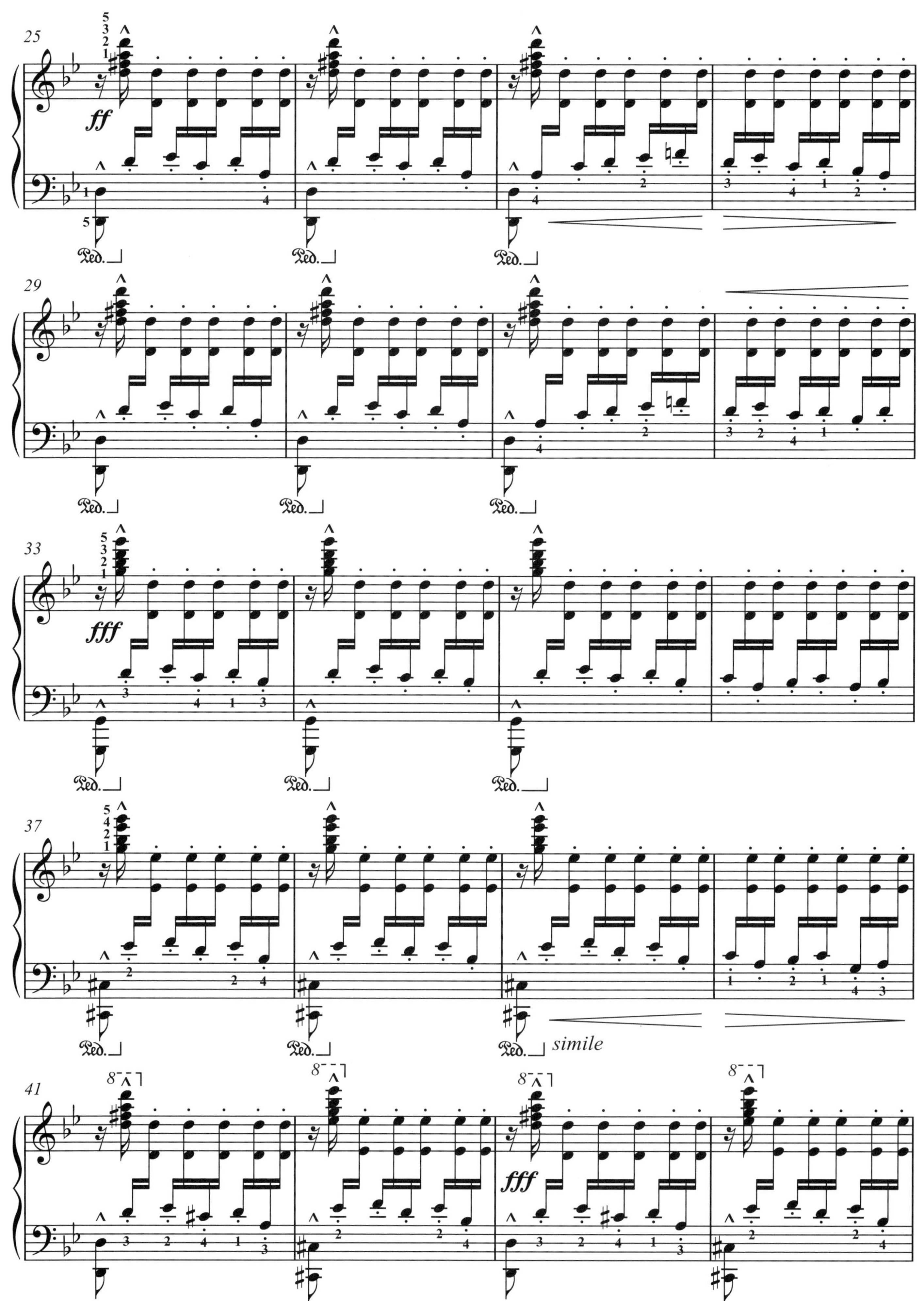
ff
fff
simile
fff

45
8
dim. poco a poco

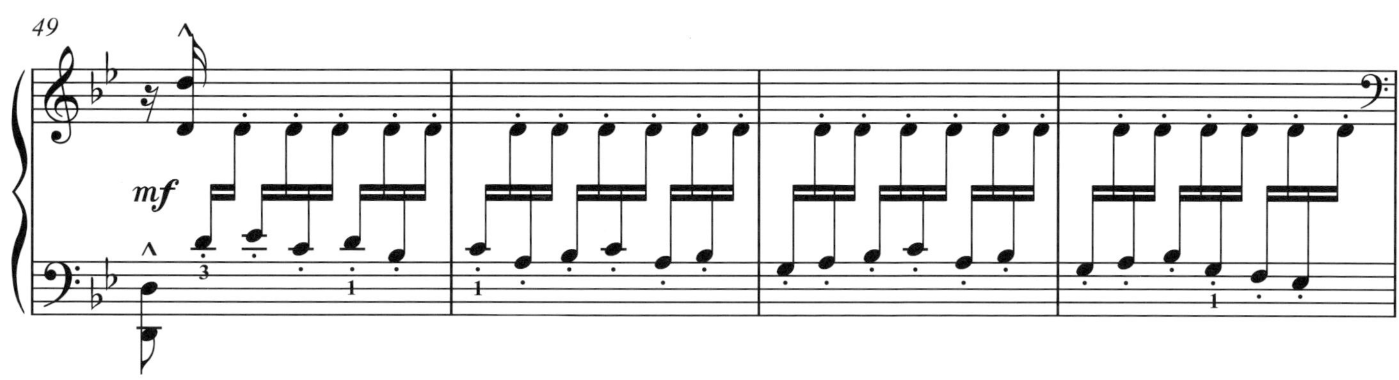
49
mf

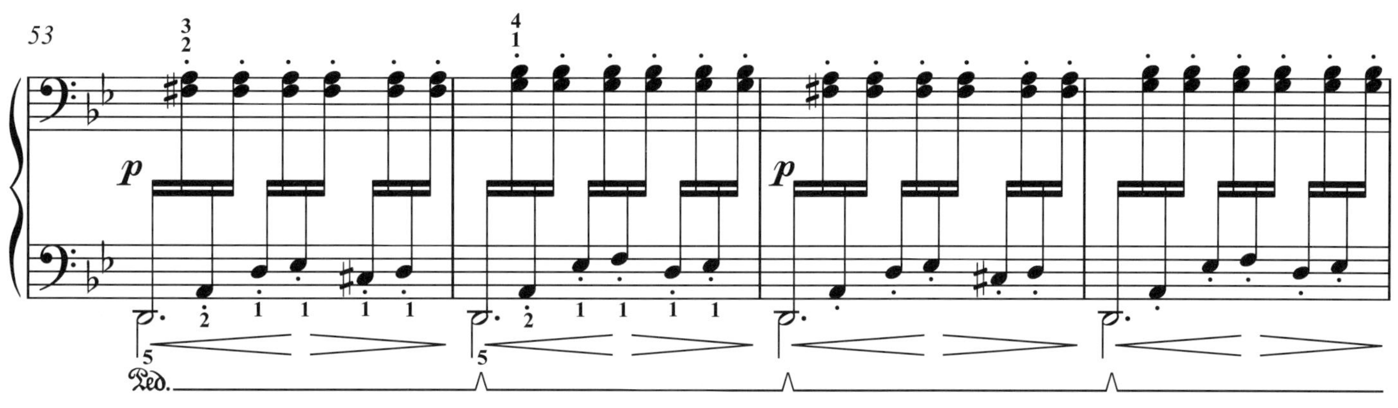
53
p
p
Ped.

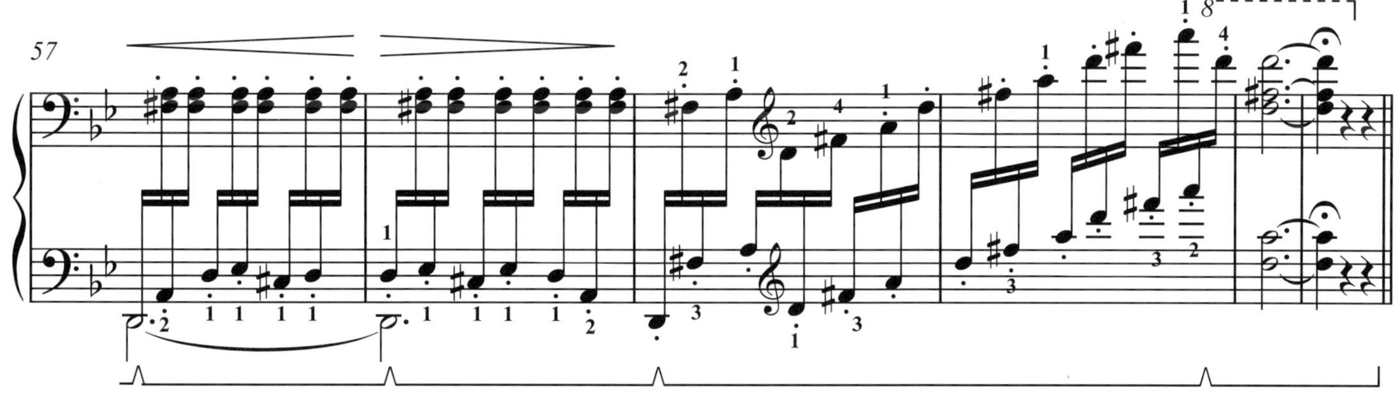
57
8

cantando largamente ma dolce
mf
poco cresc.
mf
sf dim.
mf
sf
dim. e rit. molto
rit. molto
rit. molto
dim. e rall.
marcato
marcato
molto morendo
a tempo

98
sf
dim.
cresc.
103
rit.
LH
cresc.
107
dim.
morendo
a tempo
112
rall.
115
molto rall.
p
morendo

123
Tempo I
pp
marcato il canto
127
fp
131
135
139
mf
cresc.
poco
a
poco
143

147
ff
151
sempre cresc.
155
fff
159
fff
163
8
sempre ff
167
dim.
poco
a

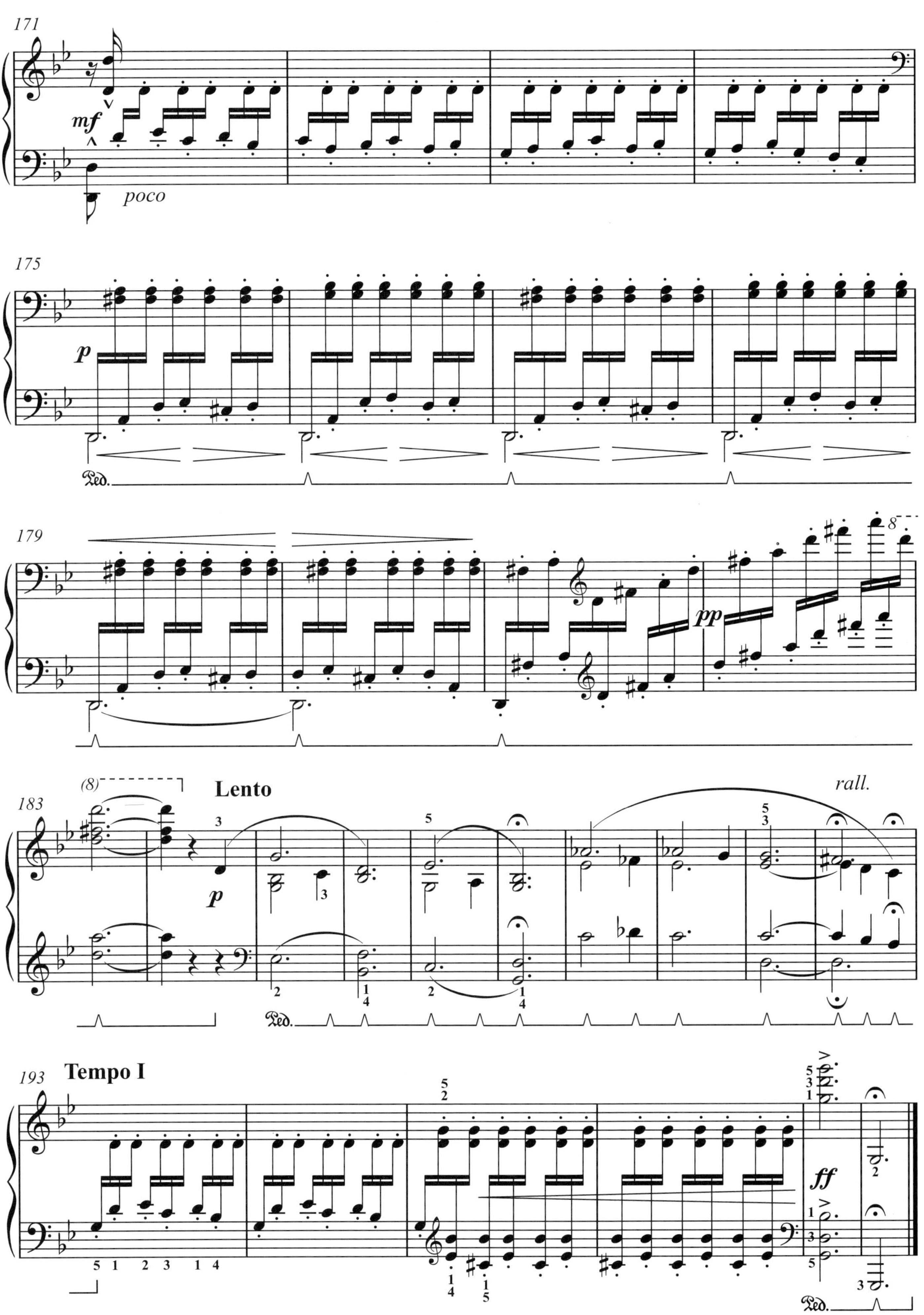
171
mf
poco
175
p
Ped.
179
pp
8
183
(8)
Lento
rall.
193
Tempo I
ff
Ped.

Prelude in G♯ minor

Sergei Rachmaninoff (1873–1943)

Set up

Key: G♯ minor
Time signature: 12/8
Tempo: Allegro:
♩. = 88–92
Style: Late Romantic
Technical Focus:
Rhythmical accompaniment pattern, finger strength and balance, *rubato*, spread chords, and melodic nuance.

During the Baroque period, a prelude was considered a preface or an introduction to a work, but in the Romantic era, it became an independent entity. Rachmaninoff's preludes contain some of his most personal writing for the instrument. This stirring yet dazzling piece features a doleful, ghostly melody set against a swirling and unsettled accompaniment.

PREPARATION

The scale and arpeggio of G♯ minor (the harmonic minor is written below) is a good place to start. Aim to practice the note patterns with the suggested fingering; work at four octave scales and arpeggios. For practice purposes, try a n*on-legato* touch for definition:

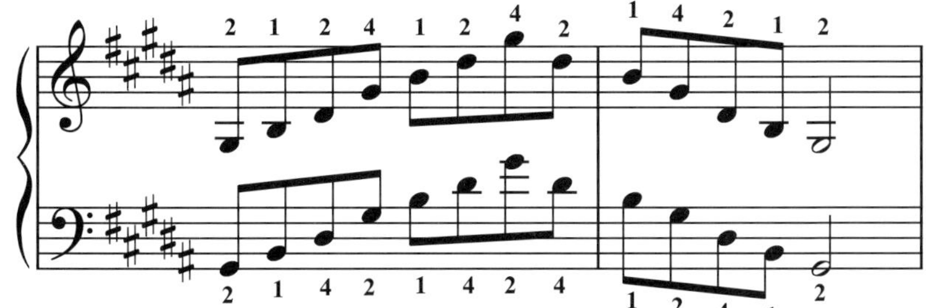

At this level it can be beneficial to play arpeggios in contrary motion patterns. Begin on the G♯ above middle C, and move outwards with both hands, returning back to the same G♯.

This prelude requires a significant amount of movement around the keyboard, particularly with regard to spread chords, which are a feature. Let's look at the chord at bar 43 (beat 1):

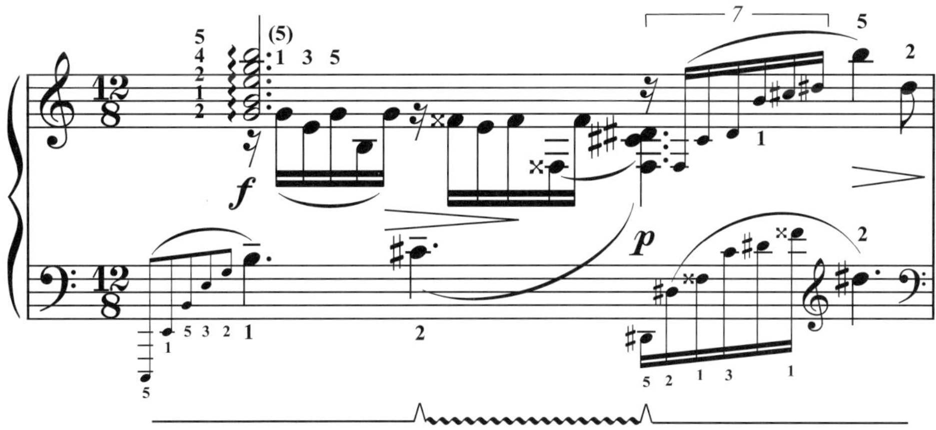

The left-hand part has already been written as a rolled chord, that is, written out as an ornamental passage, and it can be a beneficial exercise to isolate this chord. Practice hands separately; taking the left hand first, write in your preferred fingering, and play slowly, from the bottom E to top B, using a heavy touch with clearly articulated fingers. Exaggerated accents always help to develop secure finger patterns and hand positions:

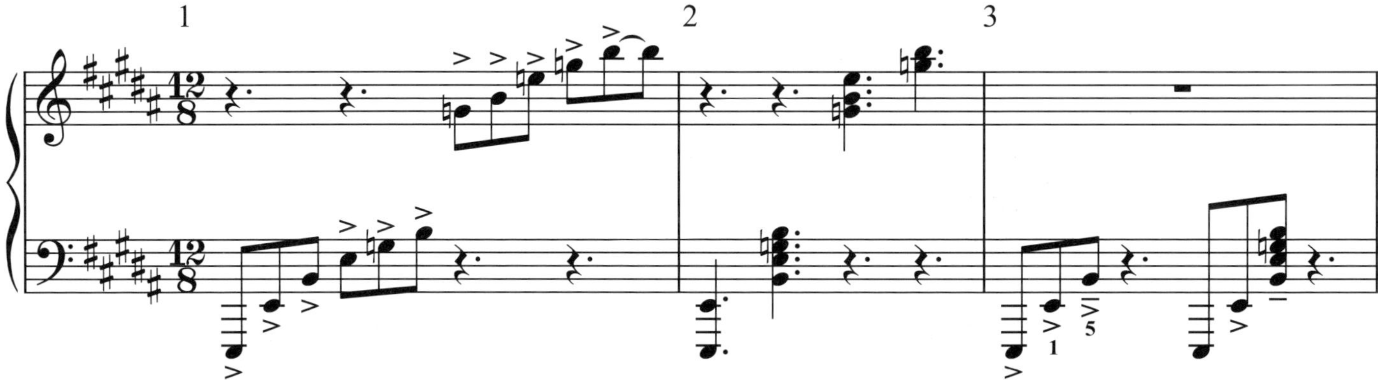

An upward 'sweeping' motion with the left hand from the first note, E, to the *tenuto* B (beat 1, sixth note), moving the whole arm lightly, in a lateral motion or sideways across the key surface, combined with a very flexible wrist, will aid fingers and help with speed too (a practice version of which is seen in example 1). Example 2 illustrates chordal practice. In example 3, the movement from the second note to the third will require spot practice, as the hand changes position; try to create a deeper, more deliberate sound on the third note, and work at the succeeding note pattern as a chord.

When applying speed to the left-hand rolled chord, use a weighted touch on the first and last notes only. You should now be able to achieve a rippled effect free of any jolts or bumps. Speed comes from the security of firmly knowing the position changes and remembering the movement needed to play them.

The right hand can be practiced in the same manner. When combining the hands, allow the left-hand pattern to sound first, feeding the right-hand chord into the sound (as written in 1 of the example). Aim to work at many of the spread chords in this way.

PRACTICE TECHNIQUES

Right-hand practice

The accompaniment figures must be fluent, rhythmical, smooth, and above all, provide a shimmering backdrop for the left-hand melody. A particular issue is the necessary power and control needed by the outer fingers to maintain the pattern and keep the pulse without tensing. Here are a few practice ideas.

Finger Strength in Patterns

The opening phrase contains this simple motif:

It uses just two notes (G♯ and D♯) which essentially appear as a chord. Experiment by using the suggested fingering (5, 3 and 1). Both the third and fifth finger will need much attention as they can be weak and unable to afford the necessary clarity needed for a sustained, even pulse.

Three elements are important:

1 A fast moving lateral wrist motion; the wrist constantly switching positions from right (photo 1) to left (photo 3) via the middle position seen in photo 2, and back, connecting the movements with constantly undulating motion, which moves swiftly from side to side, supporting the fingers. The fifth finger will benefit the most from this constant support. It helps to exaggerate movements when playing slowly:

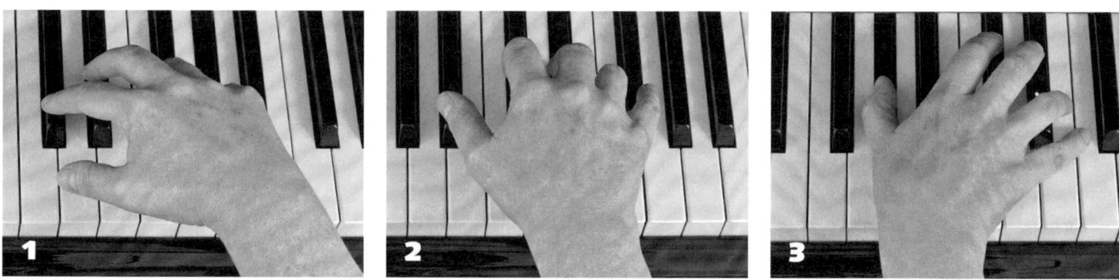

Ensure the wrist doesn't stay 'stuck' in one position, which can cause it to 'lock-up'.

2 A strong third finger acts as a pivot, allowing the thumb and fifth finger to oscillate with ease. It will need to rapidly repeat the D♯s, so must be prepared to be actively working all the time; lift it deliberately after each repetition at first, and with time, less movement will be required as the finger becomes stronger and accustomed to the feeling and the motion. The fifth finger will also benefit from attentive work; at a slow speed it needs a lot of weight behind the key, so that it is connecting deeply with each note, using the fingertip. As is often the case, accents and isolated finger practice help to develop finger strength and hand balance, but make sure you do this in short bursts without causing any pain:

3 Once the fingers know the patterns and are comfortable repeating them, tension breaks can be implemented in order to release the stiffness which can occur when any pattern is repeated. Build in places to break the tension at first, as much as once or twice per bar to begin with, and aim to use a constantly rotating wrist; small circular movements can be added to the lateral wrist motion to aid firmness in the third and fifth finger.

From bar 5, the patterns frequently change position, which offers a natural break. It can be beneficial to practice these figurations with a very heavy touch for several bars at a time, and when you return to playing the passage lightly, you should find it easier to control the notes patterns.

Tonal and rhythmic evenness are vital. Set a metronome on a sixteenth note (semiquaver) beat (possibly sixteenth note equals 160 beats per minute, at first). As speed is gradually added, so each note must still be even without any sense of rushing.

The right-hand pattern changes from bars 24–30. Play each group of sixteenth notes as a chord; you can do this separately (1) and with the left hand (2), as at bar 24:

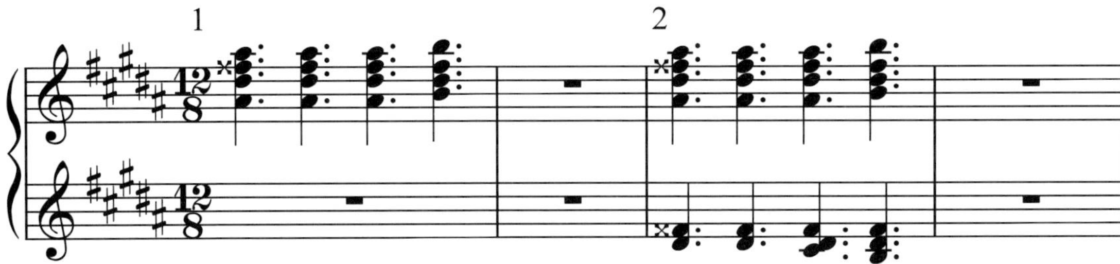

The fifth finger might require extra weight. The hand and wrist could offer support by turning the wrist slightly to the right, using arm-weight in conjunction with the forearm.

Chords at the end of bar 30, need a powerful sound leading up to bar 31, which moves towards the climax (bar 34). Focus on the top notes of each chord, giving a sense of direction, and helping to propel the music forward. Resist the temptation to rush from bars 31–34 (beat 1). Top notes in bar 32 (beats 3 and 4) will sparkle with clear accents and extra time for them to 'sound'.

Left-hand practice
The left-hand melody is like a tragic song, full of anguish, and therefore requires a penetrating timbre. Some melody notes (bars 2–14), contain *tenuto* markings (such as bar 3, beat 1 and bar 4, beat 4); in order for the sound to carry through longer beats, such as the E at bar 6, beat 3, the fingertips will benefit from making a 'special' connection with the key, depressing it into the key bed, past the escapement action, for a rich sound. Not all melody notes need this attention, but careful nuancing and melodic inflections will set this piece alight.

Melody notes at the top of rolled chords, as at bar 4, beat 4, and bar 8, beat 1, must come to the fore, therefore reserve more power for the thumb, but resisting any urge to 'hit' the keys. Aim to 'cushion' the sound with a soft wrist and arm. Only depress the note with the help of the wrist and forearm for a full sound.

Practice the melodic material heavily, even for the softer dynamics, as you can always cut back when balancing with the right-hand accompaniment. Imagine singing the melody; where would you inject more colour? Each phrase is like a sentence, so where will you put the most emphasis? For example, the first phrase (bars 2–8), should ideally be softer than the second (bars 9–16). How will you convey this to your audience? It can be more productive to think about this as learning commences.

Bars 15–20 contain some challenging passages for the left hand, especially for those with smaller hands. The downward arpeggio figures (last beat of bar 16, 17, 18 and 19) require spot practice.

Work at each sixteenth note pattern separately: firstly, the figure appears as written (in the example); 1 assesses the movement needed via two chords; Nos. 2 and 3 works at moving across a wide interval at speed. Use a large lateral wrist and arm motion for No. 4, so that all notes can be played *legato*, accenting the lower note. Now accent the top note followed by the bottom (5); repeating notes can help with articulation too. Finally, accent the middle notes (6).

Tip

The sustaining pedal forms an integral part of this piece, some of which has already been written into the score. It should be used more for sonority than obtaining *legato*, and is crucial for 'catching' the many bass-note patterns and chords which can't be joined by the fingers.

As you play the last or lowest note, move swiftly to the subsequent chord.

From bar 20, the lower dotted quarter notes (dotted crotchets) are important in the texture and must be held throughout each beat, building the sound in the chords from bar 24–30. Observe the *tenuto* markings and catch every beat with the sustaining pedal.

The reprise of the melody in bar 35 (beat 4), this time in chords, would benefit from a *legato* fingering (as has been suggested), even though a *staccato* touch is indicated. A 'soft' *non-legato* approach is appropriate for this style.

Hands together

Coordination might be a challenge in some passages. For example at bar 15, where the left hand inner voice (F×, A♯, G♯, B, C× and F×) requires judicious placing with the accompaniment (as shown by the vertical lines):

Practice the inner part alone with the right hand for security. Similarly, the subsequent four bars (16–19), could be worked at in very small increments to ensure precision.

The final two lines might need detailed slow practice. The left hand moves over the right (bars 45–46); when practicing, add accents to the right hand's D♯s in bar 46, in order to keep accurate coordination. Similarly at bar 47, if left hand G♯s are emphasised then ensemble should feel more comfortable. A brisk, regular pulse must be the ultimate aim until the last two G♯s, which can be placed with a slight *ritenuto*.

Partial Pedal Changes and Flutter Pedalling

Direct pedalling, that is, where the foot depresses the sustaining pedal as far down as is possible, releasing all the dampers, bringing it up again at the end of each beat of the bar, is often too abrupt and austere for much piano repertoire, particularly Romantic and Impressionist music. Pedal dampers need to be able to 'hover' and change frequently, although not completely, in order to continually clear the sound.

There are several areas of pedalling open to the pianist when using the sustaining pedal, possibly as many as five or six layers, depending on the instrument; from depressing the pedal fractionally, even as little as an eighth of an inch, to lowering the foot and pedal as far as it will go.

Partial pedal changes or half damping, can take place when the dampers just clear the surface of the strings and therefore the foot will not be completely depressed to the floor, but rather half way down. Partly changing the pedal will help avoid the problem of smudging or blurring harmonies.

Flutter pedalling, or 'vibrato pedalling', might be marked on the score as shown in the following example (bar 43) with a wavy line, and it refers to rapidly moving the pedal up and down to continually clear the sound, but not fully:

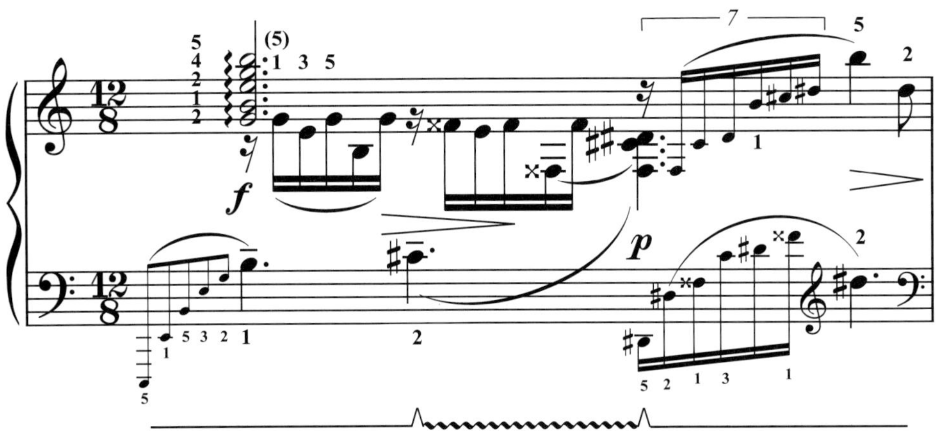

Fluttering requires quick, shallow movements with the foot, only just clearing the strings, so that full vibration will not take place. Keep your foot firmly on the sustaining pedal resisting any urge to 'hit' it, and practice a swift but regular, oscillating movement, allowing the dampers to fractionally hover over the strings, ridding the overall sound of too much blurring but creating a subtle haze.

Foot movements might need some practice; they should be as quiet as possible. Also aim to keep damper sound to a minimum as the dampers touch the strings.

Flutter and half pedalling are often not marked in a score, because the composer generally leaves it up to the performer, but I've made a few suggestions and hopefully you will be able to apply these techniques to other pieces too.

Rubato and Ritenuto

Rubato literally means 'stolen time'. In music, *rubato* gives a performer permission to shape a phrase expressively, allowing time to be taken at various points during the phrase, so the passage is played in a manner that might be termed un-rhythmical. Originally it was used in the context of expression by speeding up and slowing down the tempo, but *rubato* is often used today more liberally by composers and performers.

In Rachmaninoff's music, *rubato* offers the music a chance to breathe. I would always suggest playing rhythmically when first learning a piece, but once under the fingers, specific areas of this work require more relaxed tempos. For example, bar 37 might be more convincing (and easier to play) if a little time is taken on the fourth beat, where a rolled chord could be 'placed', that is, played a fraction slower, perhaps as much as a couple of seconds, than the tempo marking suggests.

Rachmaninoff is very specific about tempo markings throughout and the *ritenuto* appears many times, bars 3, 6, 10, etc. This is the composer's way of employing tempo changes for expressive effect. *Meno mosso* (less movement) and *accelerando* (getting faster) are also regular fixtures too.

It's tempting to take lots of time in a piece such as this, but generally a slightly more rhythmical approach is the most effective.

INTERPRETATION

Rachmaninoff's music is synonymous with brooding melodic lines and displays of emotion. Start the opening very softly, with the first note just brushing or skimming the keys; how lightly can you play? This is a good place to experiment with the sound, building quickly to the beginning of bar 2, which must be *forte*, then back again to *piano*, all within the space of two bars. There are so many possible variations on the dynamic range available here, depending on the instrument.

Prelude in G♯ minor

Op. 32 No. 12

Sergei Rachmaninoff (1873–1943)

meno mosso
poco accel.
poco rit.
meno mosso
rit.
a tempo
rit.
a tempo
dim.

21
simile
rit.
a tempo
23
dim.
pp
poco a poco cresc.
Ped.
25
simile
27
29

31
sff
33
p
ff
35
meno mosso
p
37
mf
simile
39
p
cresc.
dim.

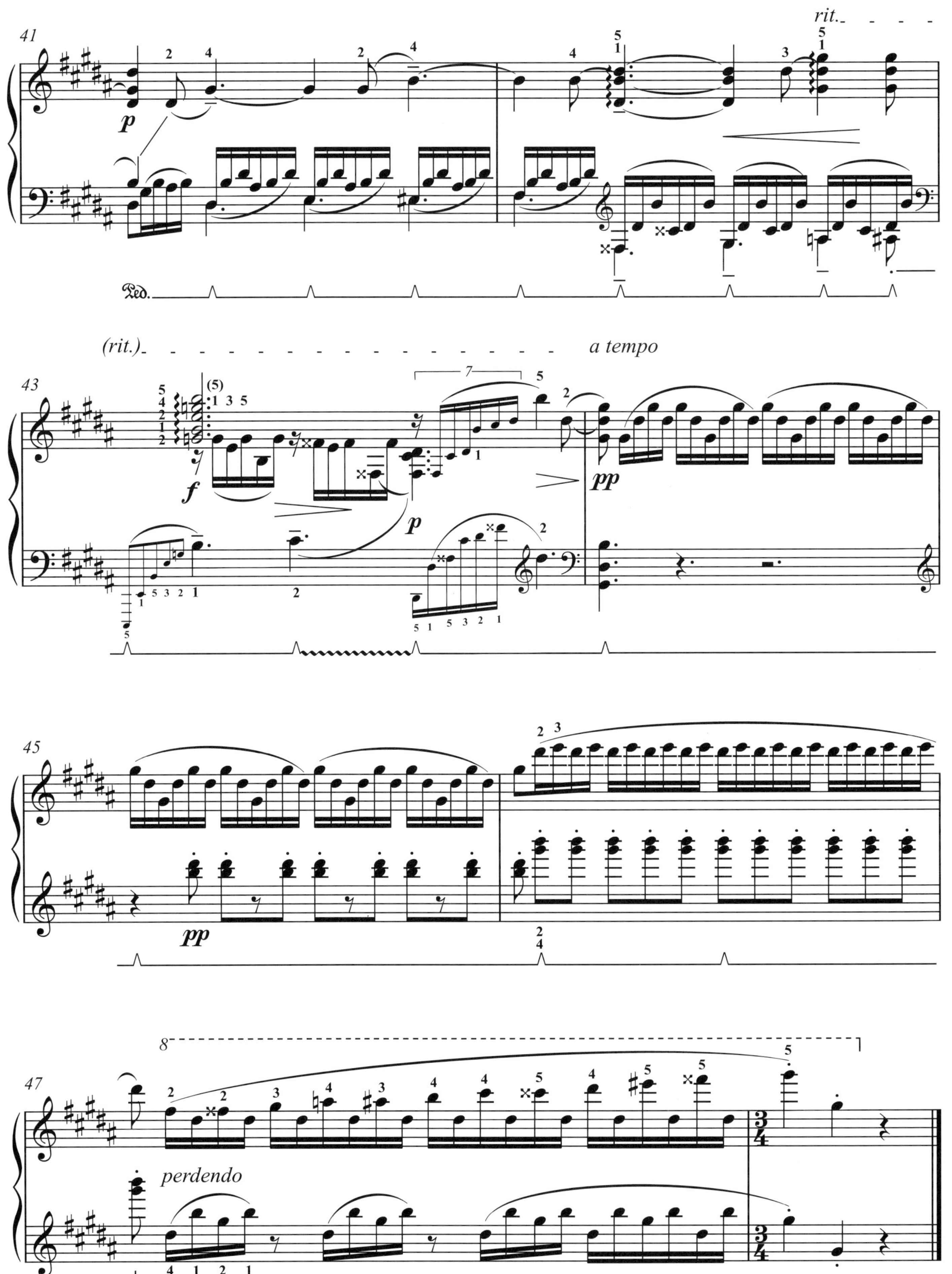

rit.
(rit.)
a tempo
perdendo

Practice Reminders

Warm-Ups

The final section of this book is devoted to warm-up exercises. Book 2 contained a small section on this subject (on page 10); here in Book 3, however, more exercises have been added.

1 Start with a posture check. Sit comfortably with a relaxed upper torso; the height of the stool must allow you to feel in control at the keyboard (see Book 1, pg. 6, for tips on posture).

2 Drop your arms by your side and encourage them to be completely floppy, with no tension at all (they will feel heavy as the muscles relax). The shoulders should also ideally be loose and not raised. Now lift your forearms, from the elbow, to the height of the keyboard; they should feel completely relaxed as you do this.

3 Play the following chord pattern, fully sounding the notes but with a relaxed wrist, arm, elbow and shoulder (it helps to consciously think about this final point), and do so until it becomes a habit; aim to 'let go' or release any tension as you hold the chords.

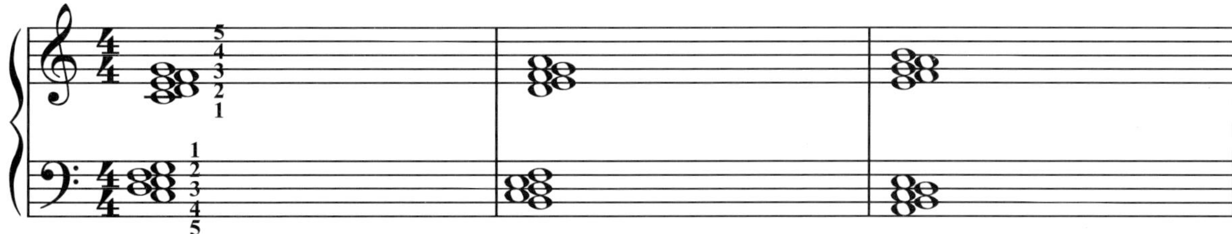

4 This short five-finger exercise in both hands, will loosen fingers. Play SLOWLY and *legato*; start with a metronome mark of ♪ = 152, increasing gradually to ♩ = 152:

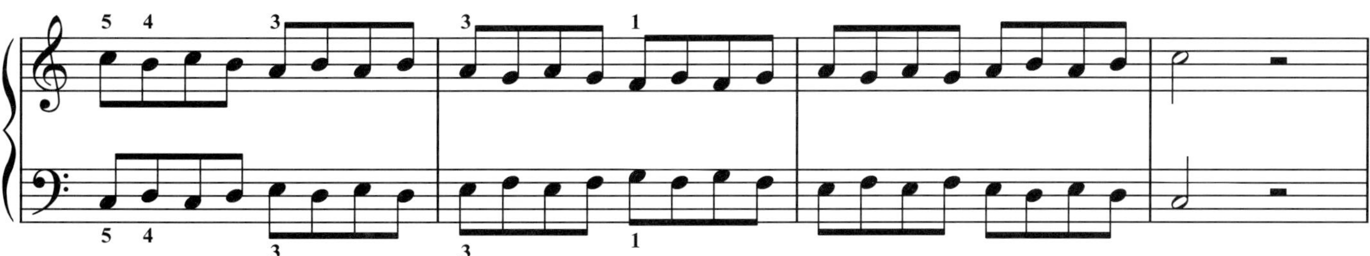

5 Now play again with a *non-legato* touch followed by a *staccato* touch. Keep relaxed when employing these touches; wrists should be pliable so they don't feel stiff.

6 The following two exercises are based on trill patterns. Start slowly, increasing the speed and pay attention to every finger and how it plays each key. Resist the urge to rush the last note of each triplet:

7 This exercise will encourage rotational or circular wrist movement (return to the image of the door knob):

8 Now let's focus on tone production, with the following chords:

Chords provide an excellent opportunity to sink into the keys, and diminished seventh chords (a chromatic chord comprising of the interval of several minor thirds) lie conveniently under the hands. Play them *legato*, keeping the notes depressed until the final second before playing the next chord. You can vary the sound and colour each time you repeat the group. Listening is vital, as well as using a free, light arm movement and arm-weight. You may also enjoy 'voicing' each chord, highlighting different notes within the chords.

There are numerous ways to warm-up but start with these exercises, and in time you can devise your own.